The
Amazing Power of Grace

LIVING, SUCCEEDING AND EXCELLING BY GRACE

HUMPHREY O. AKPARAH

Copyright © 2012 by Humphrey O. Akparah

The Amazing Power of Grace
Living By Grace
by Humphrey O. Akparah

Printed in the United States of America

ISBN 9781624194818

All rights reserved solely by the author. The author guarantees all contents are original and do not infringe upon the legal rights of any other person or work. No part of this book may be reproduced in any form without the permission of the author. The views expressed in this book are not necessarily those of the publisher.

Unless otherwise indicated, Bible quotations are taken from The from The Holy Bible, King James Version. Copyright © 1972 by Thomas Nelson Inc., Camden, New Jersey 08103; The New King James Version NKJV. Copyright 1979, 1980, 1982 by Thomas Nelson, Inc. Used by permission; The HOLY BIBLE, NEW INTERNATIONAL VERSION,. Copyright © 1973, 1978, 1984 by International Bible Society. Used by permission of Zondervan Publishing House; The NEW AMERICAN STANDARD BIBLE® NAS. Copyright © 1960, 1962, 1963, 1971, 1972, 1973, 1975, 1977, 1995 by The Lockman Foundation, LaHabra, CA Used by permission; *The Message Remix 2.0 MSG: The Bible in Contemporary Language Navpress.* Kindle Edition; The Living Bible TLB. Copyright © 1971 by Tyndale House Publishers, Wheaton, Illinois 60187; and *The Amplified Bible* AMP, *containing the amplified Old Testament and the amplified New Testament.* Copyright © 1987 by The Lockman Foundation: La Habra, CA.

www.xulonpress.com

Acknowledgment

This book will not be complete without my acknowledging all those who helped me especially with the proof-reading and editing. After writing the book I knew I needed competent people; friends and ministers of the gospel to proof-read and edit it. I was humbled by the responses of these great men and women of God and their willingness in spite of their very busy schedules to proof-read and edit the book. These include: Pastor Bob Johnston, Senior Pastor, Pastor Godfrey Adderley, Associate Pastor, Global kingdom Ministries, Scarborough, Ontario. Barrister (Mrs.) Oluyemisi Abrahams LLB, Barrister, Solicitor and Notary, Pickering Ontario. Others are: Rod Woolbridge, a friend that sticks closer than a brother; my manager at Goodwill Employment Services who prefers to be anonymous but without whose constant encouragement, push and reminders this book would've taken longer to come. Lastly, my daughter Chidinma who was with me everyday and helped to proof-read the manuscripts.

Table of Contents

Acknowledgment v
Chapter 1 What Is Grace? 9
Chapter 2 Types of Grace 14
Chapter 3 Living by Grace 22
Chapter 4 Grace Adventures 31
Chapter 5 The Grace Driven Life 40
Chapter 6 The Origin of Grace 47
Chapter 7 People Who Lived by Grace 55
Chapter 8 Those Who Lost Their Grace 66
Chapter 9 Fear, Anxiety and Worry 78
Chapter 10 God's Antidote 94
Chapter 11 Grace in Sin: Grace for sinners 104
Chapter 12 Vision Driven Grace Life 115
Chapter 13 Grace for the Dying 123
Chapter 14 The Joy of Living by Grace 131
Chapter 15 Grace to Change Your
              Circumstances 142
Chapter 16 The Grace Chapter 157

Chapter 1

*H*ow would you like to hear these words everyday, "My grace is sufficient for you, for my strength is made perfect in weakness?" How would you like to live daily in active grace and in favor with God and man? What would your life look like if it was driven by grace?

This revelation came as I was searching for something else unrelated to grace in the scripture, when suddenly; something hit my mind as never before. When reading in 2 Corinthians 12:9, this verse jumped out at me and I couldn't get past it: "My grace is sufficient for you, for my strength is made perfect in weakness." I paused and read it over and over again the impression of it was so strong. I knew God wanted to speak to me through this scripture. So I stopped and said, "Lord, what do you want to say to me?" I listened as the idea to write a book on GRACE came flooding through my spirit. Immediately, I took a sheet of paper and jotted down the table of contents as it was being given to me and, instantly, I jumped to my computer and started typing.

What is Grace?

The first purpose of this book is to glorify Jesus Christ who gave me the grace and inspiration to write it, and secondly, to discuss the subject of grace in great detail as a recipient of this wonderful gift. It is my hope and prayer that all who read this book would appreciate, and begin to experience the peace, contentment and joy of knowing that the grace of God is with you no matter who you are, and no matter what your circumstances and situations have been. Grace follows you wherever you go and in whatever you do, even when you do not know that it exists. No one can truly comprehend the full implications of this subject. It is as vast and encompassing as God Himself. Grace is dispensed to everyone according to the measure of God's gifting to each individual, not according to your desire (although you can receive more grace if you ask for it).

Grace is an attribute of the Divine nature and therefore, beyond our human finite capacity to fully comprehend it. I humbly ask you to keep an open mind while reading this book so that you will come to a fuller understanding of how grace works and how it's been working in your life for a long time without your knowledge. I pray you will see how abundantly you have been receiving and living in the grace of God by the little things that have gone unnoticed through the years! Finally, I want you to learn how you can live daily in the abundance of God's grace. You will surely be blessed even before you get to the end of this book. Happy reading!

Grace as a noun, according to the Oxford English Dictionary, is:

Chapter 1

- An attractive quality of movement that is smooth, elegant and controlled.
- Quality of behavior that is polite and pleasant and deserves respect.
- The kindness that God shows toward the human race.

From the Thesaurus, grace means: attractiveness, beauty, charm, elegance, courtesy, fineness, loveliness, polish, refinement, virtue, beautiful, decorate, garnish, glory, honor, dignify, loveliness, benefaction, charity, compassion, favor, forgiveness, generosity, goodness, goodwill, kindness, love, mercy, pardon, blessing, etc. These are special nouns, adjectives and verbs that describe God's special attributes. He also bestows them on humans to beautify us, inspire our work, brighten our day, and enrich our lives here on earth. It is a quality that beautifies us, makes us special and unique; it differentiates us from everything and everyone else. It is designed and released, as necessary or upon request, to make our sufferings and troubles in this world lighter or easier to bear. It is not meant to remove us completely from the problems of this cruel world, but it is meant to soften them so that they are palliative to our trials and agonies here on earth.

Since the beginning God has used grace to deal with the erring human race. When Adam and Eve sinned in the Garden of Eden and hid themselves from Him, they realized that God was displeased with them; God responded first with grace and mercy. God killed an animal and used its skin to cover their nakedness, and to protect them from the shame and humiliation that the devil intended for them. The scripture says, "God commanded His love toward us, in that, while we were yet sinners, Christ died for us" (Romans 5:8). Grace is all about God's love and concern for our welfare and this brings us to the popular definition of grace.

Definition

The popular definition of grace, as we all know, is: "the unmerited favor of God." I would add—grace is God's unmerited favor bestowed on the undeserving human race. This underscores the fact that no one deserves or receives more favor from God than you, for we all stand condemned before a holy and just God. None should boast of whatever gifts or blessings we receive from God. By the same token, none of us has the right to complain, criticize or question God for what we did or did *not* receive because grace is a gift that we did not merit or deserve in the first place.

Paul, the faithful apostle, said, "For I say, through the grace given to me, to everyone that is among you, not to think of himself more highly than he ought to think; but to think soberly according to how God has dealt to everyone a measure of faith" (Romans 12:3). Rather than complain, God has given us the right and grace to ask for whatever we need or lack. With God we can ask for anything. It is His prerogative to determine what is acceptable and what is not.

His gift of grace is available just for the asking. The reaches of God's grace are beyond human imagination. So why not take advantage of this free gift and ask now, for the virtues, blessings, help, healing and any other blessings you want from God. I'm sure He will hear you. The scripture says, "For the grace of God that brings salvation has appeared to all men" (Titus 2: 11). That means, this is your time, the moment you have been waiting for, to

Chapter 1

receive from God the grace you did not know was there for you.

Grace has also been described in these acronyms as: **G**od's **R**iches **A**t **C**hrist's **E**xpense.

>   **G** - God's
>   **R** - Riches
>   **A** - At
>   **C** - Christ's
>   **E** – Expense

God's gift of Jesus Christ is the highest grace that God has given to the world. Christ is the fullness of the Godhead in a human or bodily form, "For in Him (Christ) dwells all the fullness of the Godhead bodily" (Colossians 2:9). Living by grace is appreciating all that God has given to you freely, which if He had required payment, you would be in jail by now, dead and gone. Living by grace is appreciating God's gift of Jesus Christ to you who paid the price for your sins.

Grace is the unction to function.

Chapter 2

Types of Grace

Most people do not realize that there are several different types of grace: active and passive grace, hidden and obvious grace, present and past grace, early and late grace, primary and secondary grace, masculine and feminine grace, sustainable or abiding grace, unsustainable grace, and living and dying grace. I could go on because the list is inexhaustible. All these forms of grace are there just for the asking. You only have to know what you are lacking or missing. Then ask and it will be granted to you according to the will and purpose of the Giver.

The scripture says, "Therefore, I say to you, what things so ever you desire, when you pray, believe that you will receive them and you shall have them" (Mark 11:24). Another translation says, "Therefore I say to you, whatever thing you ask when you pray, believe that you will receive them and you will have them" (Mark 11:24 NKJV). James 1:5 says, "If any of you lack wisdom, let him ask of God, who gives to all men liberally and without reproach and it will be given him." In the same vein, I say to my readers, if anyone lacks *grace* in any area of life, let him ask of God who gives to all men without reproach and it will be given him. The scripture does not make distinctions between men and women so this verse and all other scriptures apply to both men and women alike. Now let us expound on these different types of grace.

Active Grace: What is active grace? Active grace is present in your life now whether you know it or not. Many people are ignorant of active grace in their lives and so do not praise God for it. Others may use active grace as a thing of pride and boasting; some even use it to afflict others by cheating, swindling people, and perpetrating wickedness on their victims.

Active grace is the grace you have right now that helps you to live your life. It is the sum total of all the different kinds of grace that are operating in you– *at present time*. Not all of them are continuous or sustainable, so they will come and go. While they are active, you use them and they beautify and uplift you; they make your life tick. They bring joy, peace, love, and favor to you in the present because they are actively operating in your life right now. But make no mistake about it, grace may cease one day.

A complicated network of different kinds of grace runs throughout our lives. They sometimes come as a package at birth, or they are added to us as we need or ask for them. Every grace can be extended or increased in measure. Therefore, you should be able to list the graces that are currently operating in your life or those that you wish to have. You must begin to ask for them. Some examples of active grace include: beauty, favor, health, wisdom, eloquence or the gift-of-gab, and other natural endowments that define your life. They must be natural to qualify as gifts of grace.

Passive Grace: Passive grace is the grace that is no longer active, but rather docile or subdued in your life right now. It could be that it was once active but now is dormant or quiescent. Sometimes passive grace lies dormant because of lack of use or lack of appreciation of its virtues and values in your life. Remember that everything you receive from the Divine is for a purpose and reason. Passive grace can be made active again by use or by asking for its restoration. The good thing about passive grace is that you do not need to re-learn to use it when it is restored. Passive grace can be taken away for good especially if it is not appreciated. It may be thought of as a curse instead of a blessing and it may be used to commit evil. As I said earlier, "Every grace has a purpose."

Obvious Grace: Obvious graces are those natural gifts that are glaringly clear and immediately obvious to the eyes, ears, and other senses. You do not need to be told or wait long to find out that a person has these gifts. Obvious gifts attest to God's kindness and blessing upon an individual. It is not meant to be misused, placed as a stumbling block for others to cause them to fall or fail, or to elevate the recipient above other individuals. But God gives to everyone a measure of grace just to make him or her different from all other things on earth that He has made. To Mr. A God gives more of this grace here and more of another grace there to Miss 'B'. They are in different proportions and order so that no one has it all, and no one is left without any. God is the God of variety and He distributes to each one of us graces and gifts according to His purpose, pleasure, and the work He has assigned for us to do here on earth.

Obvious grace can include beauty, intelligence, physical strength, wealth, eloquence, technical skills, creativity, leadership, and voice quality. Although wealth is not a natural grace, wealth can be inherited at birth. The recipient receives it as a natural gift or endowment just as any other natural gift is received. It then forms or becomes part of the person's network of graces at birth that helps him/her become who they are or would be. However, some obvious graces such as beauty, voice quality, wealth, and physical strength have become subject to abuse and pride. Some who possess them do not see them as gifts of grace, but use them to intimidate, maltreat, castigate, and abuse others. Those were not God's intended purpose for giving such grace. God intends for the recipients to use them to glorify Him, edify and comfort others, and help mitigate people's suffering. He did not intend for the rich to continue to get richer at the expense of the poor or to provoke the less privileged to envy and jealousy, to kill or to commit suicide. God gave gifts and graces to beautify humanity and to receive praises for His work and wisdom.

Are you using the grace which you freely received to help your neighbors and humanity at large? Remember that the gifts are not your own; they are only gifts for specific assignments and they can be taken away if the Giver thinks you are not using them for His intended purposes.

Living by grace is using all your gifts of grace for their intended purposes. If you do not know the purposes of your gifts, please discuss this with your pastor or seek wise counsel. Look around and see if you can identify God's grace in the lives of others.

Hidden Grace: Hidden graces are those finer, inner qualities of life that make one graceful, inwardly beautiful, and strong even when the outward is weak and not so attractive. Hidden grace comes with much spiritual strength and beauty. It is the type of grace that keeps the weak and poor going strong when even the rich and mighty fall and fail. It is the grace that continues when all hope is lost. To some people, hidden grace is preferred above obvious graces, and in the sight of God, they are priceless and sometimes indispensable.

Hidden graces include love, joy, peace, humility, contentment, faith, hope and patience. Others included on this list are cheerfulness, helpfulness, optimism, simplicity, courage, and integrity. Hidden graces are not obvious, and are often not appreciated. In fact, sometimes they are looked down upon, despised, and rejected. Many times those who possess these graces are taken advantage of, cheated and robbed, but I want them to know that those graces are far more valuable than many obvious gifts, and should not be taken lightly. The scripture calls them the fruit of the Spirit. Galatians 5:22 states: "But the fruit of the Spirit is love, joy, peace, longsuffering, kindness, goodness, faithfulness, gentleness, and self-control. Against such there is no law."

Present Grace: Present grace is the grace that is current, active, and operational in your life. Present grace could be enduring or permanent or it could be transitory. When present grace is permanent it remains with you until you die. You can activate it anytime. You can even use it in a dream to your advantage. Present grace is what makes your life what it is today, but it is not guaranteed for tomorrow unless it is also permanent. Present grace is the totality of your physical, emotional, intellectual, spiritual, psychological, and physiological makeup. Unless you continue to ask for more grace in those areas you feel you need them most, or areas in which you feel most vulnerable without them, you may lose them. When you ask, you will receive.

Past Grace: Past graces are graces that you had and lost, or are no longer operative in your life after many trials. Some past graces are dead and long gone and can never be retrieved or restored. Others can be restored by use, through intercessory prayer or both. However, the scripture says, "All things are possible to him that believes" (Mark 9:23). You can take God at His word and receive back your past or dead gifts. No one should write himself off until death, because God is able to resurrect any Lazarus from the dead even after many days in the grave. After all, God allowed Abraham and Sarah to have Isaac even when they were well past the age of childbearing.

> *Therefore, it is by faith that it might be by grace... who against hope believed in hope, that he might become the father of many nations and being not weak in faith, he did not consider his own body already dead (since he was about a hundred years old), and the deadness of Sarah's womb. He did not waiver from his promise to God through unbelief, but was strong in faith giving glory to God, and being fully convinced that what he had promised he was able to perform.* (Romans 4:21)

Another translation (KJV) said he did not stagger at the promise of God through unbelief. This passage may be speaking to someone who has not yet received the grace of early childbearing. God is able to give you a mid-life or late childbearing grace. He has been doing it for ages. Believe His Word and call upon Him and expect that He will answer.

Transitory Grace: Transitory graces are those graces that come, develop, blossom, and die or go away. They are transient and not sustainable over time. Transitory grace, for example, could be like some children who are born with early childhood beauty and charm, and as they grow older, they begin to lose those attributes. By adulthood they have almost completely lost these earlier characteristics of beauty and charm. Beauty, wealth and physical strength are among graces that are transitory. However, some of these are sustained over a long time, and even become permanent, especially, if they are put to good and praise-worthy use and glorify God, the Giver.

Early and Late Grace: Many early graces can be received from birth and are developed or received early in life. Early graces could be permanent or transitory. Early graces are the building blocks for later life. If well nurtured, they help make a person grow and mature into a vibrant adult in their later years. But if not properly nurtured, they can be destroyed or become agents of self-destruction or the destruction of others. Early graces in children should be a sign of responsibility to parents, not only when graces are negative, such as sickness, but also when they are positive and strength related. Early graces, both positive and negative, can be managed and nurtured to become strengths and blessings. In other words, we can turn what appears to be a negative into a positive. Even the best graces can be misused and turned from positive to negative. Many early graces can be transitory. That is why they should be guarded with due diligence. "Guard your heart with all diligence, for out of it springs the issues of life. Your life is shaped by your thoughts" (Proverbs 4:22-23).

Conversely, some children are not born with such early graces but develop them as they grow older. Some may not even develop these finer qualities and graces until they are well past their thirties and into their early forties. Some people do not become somebody *important* in life until they are well into their fifties or sixties. There is no timeline for God to release or remove graces, but He distributes them as He sees fit for the grand purpose of His design.

Chapter 3

Living by Grace

Living by grace is the most amazing way to grow up on earth. The grace of God is completely awesome and inexhaustible. It is this life that Jesus came to give to the world. Living by grace displays a life of peace, joy, contentment, and fulfillment. It's a life of supernatural provision and abundance (see John 10:10).

- It is living by the power and will of God.
- It is living by the mercies of the Creator.
- It is living by the provisions of the All-Sufficient One.
- It is living by the goodness of the One who loves you and cares for you whether you believe in Him or not.
- It is living in the Divine blue print of your life and destiny.
- It is living by His infinite source and supply.
- It is living in Oneness with the Creator and the universe of Christ.

Living by Grace

The grace of God is the love of God made and tailored to fit your particular life and situation. Whether you know it or believe it, you have been living by grace. Furthermore, you will always and forever live by grace until you die. If you continuously reject or refuse to acknowledge and give thanks to the One who gives this gift of grace, you will receive no more.

Grace was released to the world after Jesus ascended. Our sins are now forgiven just for the asking. We can now claim and relate to God, the Omnipotent, as our Father and actually enjoy a living, loving one-on-one relationship with Him. Grace unites us with God without any condemnation of past or present sins, circumstances of birth or any other limiting or inhibiting factors. Jesus paved the way for us to live by grace and in favor with God and man (see Romans 5:1-2).

Living by grace is living with the assurance that the Higher Power above is looking after you with favor and without condemnation. Your mistakes are covered or forgiven, because He loves you by His grace and not because of who you are. God's grace covers every aspect of your life from conception, birth and up until death. You exist because while millions of other sperm raced for a connection during conception one alone survived. All others died (unless your mother had twins or triplets etc.). That alone is a testimony that you began your journey through life with the grace of God. Just because things are not working out as you planned or thought they would does not mean there is no more grace for other things and other areas of your life. There is so much grace out there you will never be able to exhaust it during your lifetime. Keep your eyes on Jesus and start reaching out to Him; more importantly, start asking for His grace now.

The Grace Life

The grace life is a life of active trust. Trusting in a superior God who is able and willing to help, provide, protect, defend, rescue, supply, maintain, intervene, comfort, uphold, sustain, bless, hear and respond, love, care, appreciate, show favor, go before, behind, above, beneath, beside, surround, uplift, and deliver you completely. God will, and is able to, restore the years that the cankerworms, caterpillars, the palmerworms, the locust, sickness, disease, divorce, poverty, famine, wars within and without have destroyed. God is able to make your life beautiful again. God is able to make even more graces abound in you.

The grace life is a life filled with enthusiasm, hope and eagerness to believe and take God at His word. It is a life of satisfaction, contentment, and inner peace. It is a life devoid of pride and strife and full of inner peace and joy. It is a life that recognizes strengths, weaknesses and limitations, but it also depends on the God of all grace to supply our needs. A grace-full life does not direct us to strife, cheating, stealing, killing, and envy to get what we desire. Doesn't God know what you need? The scripture says, "Seek ye first the kingdom of God and his righteousness and all these things shall be added unto you" (Matthew 6:33).

How to Receive Grace

> *Let us therefore come boldly unto the throne of grace that we may obtain mercy and find grace to help in time of need.* (Hebrews 4:16)

Living by Grace

The only way to receive more grace is to ask. But before you ask you must come boldly to God. Before you can come boldly, you have to establish a relationship with Him and boldly approach God's Throne of Grace. You do not come with fear, you do not come with doubt, and you do not come with unbelief. You must come believing and trusting. You must come with high hopes and expectations to receive. When God says something, He wants you to take Him at His word because He cannot lie or fail. He said that it is easier for heaven and earth to pass away than for His Word to fail. "Heaven and earth will pass away but my Word will by no means pass away" (Luke 21:33).

To obtain grace, you need mercy. *Mercy,* according to the *Oxford Advanced Learners Dictionary* means, "A kind and forgiving attitude toward somebody that you have the power to harm or right to punish." The whole concept of grace is predicated on the mercy of God toward man. God is All Powerful, All Knowing, and All Mighty. He made us, controls us, and has everything that we need. He is our source and supply. He gave us life and everything we have or received at birth. He assigned parents for us, gave us our country of origin, our race, and skin color. He gave us every basic thing with which we came into this world. He sent us to His world to live, enjoy, and populate it. The exact time and experiences of our entrance into this world is not recorded in our memory, but God is keenly aware of every intricate detail. In the same way, He created us with a plan, and purposed us to fulfill that plan knowing that we would need His help along the way.

When we rebel–as we all do–and forsake our mandates in pursuit of our own pleasures, we anger Him. Romans 3:23 says, "For all have sinned and come short of the glory of God." In the process, we mess up, muddle up, entangle ourselves, and lose our way through the maze of life. When the devil arrests us because we have encroached into his illegal territory, we get in trouble and need a Savior, an advocate or an attorney.

At this point, many people begin to curse or hate God, and embrace Satan whose promises of freedom actually sound pretty good. The catch is that they must abandon God's will and purposes and serve only Satan. Thereafter, they are thoroughly and fully brainwashed by Satan and his agents; they become his servants and do whatever he asks them to do. But they soon discover that they have been deceived and tricked by the devil and begin to look for ways of escape. They begin to devise their own forms of righteousness that obviously fall short of the God's standards.

While all of this has been happening, God in His infinite mercy has been seeking ways to help, deliver, and rescue them. When they find the grace and mercy that God has for those who trust Him, and the many promises that they have been missing, they begin the process of coming back to God. This process goes on for as long as it takes the person to reconnect with God.

At this point, we must repent of our sins and ask God to forgive us and invite Jesus into our hearts. God, looking down with mercy and kindness in His heart, will shower His blessings upon us. Like early morning dew, the grace of salvation flows through our heart and we surrender and are saved. "For by grace are you saved through faith and that not of yourselves; it is the gift of God lest any man should boast" (Ephesians 2: 8-9).

After we have been restored to the household of God and fellowship with Jesus, we receive all the rights and privileges of *sonship* in the kingdom of God. Our Father

God, through Jesus His Son and the guidance of the Holy Ghost, expects us to come boldly and freely to the Throne of Grace. There we obtain His mercy and grace to aid us with our needs, problems, desires, and ambitions. Unfortunately many of us stop short of our potential. Many of us never move beyond the joy of salvation. A walk with God is a progressive and unending life of inner peace, joy, and contentment.

When we return to God, we are made anew and declared to be the empowered sons and daughters of God. He sends forth the Spirit of His Son into our hearts and we receive the privilege to call Him Father, and He will call us His beloved children (see Galatians 4:6). Now we are no longer slaves to sin and Satan. We are new creations because we are born again in Christ Jesus and God now declares, "If any man is in Christ He is a new creation: old things are passed away; and behold all things are become new" (2 Corinthians 5:17). The adoption process is now complete and God expects us to come boldly unto the Throne of Grace to enjoy His presence and ask for whatever we need.

Because God looks down on us with mercy and favor, we will receive additional gifts of grace. He wants us to humble ourselves before Him and He will look down on us with mercy. "Humble yourselves, therefore, under the mighty hand of God, that He may exalt you in due time" (1 Peter 5:6). As He looks down with mercy, His graceful face shines on us with *the* measure of grace that we deserve. The cycle is complete. We will then be able to go in and out of the Throne Room as often as we wish. When this process is omitted, it is possible to remain in the church for a long time without once appearing at the Throne of Grace. One of the graces received from birth is the grace to call on the many names of God at anytime during our lifetime. Whenever we call out to God in truth and sincerity, He always answers regardless of the circumstances. However, until we make peace with His Son, Jesus Christ, access to the Throne of Grace is denied.

My Early Childhood

My own experience of living by grace started when I was a child. I was born and raised in a small town called Akwete, in Abia, a state in Nigeria. I was the second child of three siblings and the only boy. My parents were of humble means. We lived in a thatch-roofed, mud house. There was no electricity, no pipe-borne water, and few modern conveniences. Oftentimes my father was not at home. He was either at work in the big cities, or was not available at the time I needed him.

Because our house had a thatched roof, it often leaked when it rained. My mother was a humble, uneducated woman and in those desperate days, when it rained or when we did not have enough to eat, I would hear her weeping in the middle of the night. I also heard her praying to God to send us help. Many times I witnessed her rejoicing after a sale of her hand-woven, traditional Akwete cloth or when she received unexpected and pleasant answers to her prayers. So I learned the virtue of praying and trusting in God. Growing up and finding that I had no one on this earth I could count on to help me, I turned to God for His help with everything that I needed. So at a very early age I began to seek God on my own. I would pray for any and every need.

I began to witness miracles and answers to prayers. I did not know they were miracles at the time. I only knew that things were surprisingly happening in my favor. One of the earliest miracles I can remember vividly was the calming of violent windstorms. I grew up near the Niger Delta area of Nigeria where the rain forest brought violent wind, thunder and lightening storms during the rainy season. At times, they were so violent that they would blow off whole roofs from buildings, destroy significant parts of houses, and often expose houses to serious erosion. Our house was right at the edge of the erosive waterway. Whenever it rained during the day, we would be busy trying to hedge our home from being irreparably damaged from the foundation. My father would try to find mats or used roofing sheets to cover areas that had been blown off or significantly torn away by the windstorms.

When it rained during the night and my father was not at home, my mother found basins and plates or anything that held water to keep our mats from becoming soaking wet. We stayed up those nights moving from one room to another; from one end of the house to another while seeking an area that was dry enough for our mats. Seldom did sleep come during the storms.

Learning To Live By Grace

I was always afraid of the rainy season in my hometown because it meant suffering and misery. But it was also a time of learning to pray and trust God. When it began to thunder, lightening and rain, I would start to pray and tell God, in my own childish way, to let the wind stop or the rain go away because I did not want to see my mother crying in the middle of the night. Sometimes, to my surprise, within a short time, the rain would either stop or lessen in its intensity. Other times, it would rain so hard and furiously that I thought that we might die. However, God in His infinite mercy sustained us. When I became aware that my prayers were being answered to a large extent, I became emboldened to pray more, and to pray for other bigger and different things. Up to this point, I had not told anybody about the answers to my prayers because I did not know they were miracles and felt nobody would believe me.

Chapter 4

Grace Adventure Stories

Grace Adventure One

When I was about eleven or twelve years old, I lived in a city called Enugu which was then the capital city of Eastern Nigeria. I decided to become more adventurous because I didn't want to be a burden on my parents. I decided to venture into a small business to raise money to buy the kind of shoes and clothing I liked. My parents could not afford my tastes except on special occasions like Easter, Christmas, and New Year celebrations. I decided to use my holiday periods to trade. I chose to sell oranges but I did not have any money with which to start the business. Nobody trusted me or any child for that matter, to start a business. Money was scarce in those days. However, my elder sister, Augusta, always had money because she was very pretty and intelligent. At the age of twelve, she passed her First School Leaving Certificate exam with distinction. People who visited our house gave her money or bought her a gift. I had no real gifts so I did not receive anything close to what she had. I decided to secretly borrow six pennies from her and promised to pay her back with interest when I came back. We got along very well.

My mother allowed me to go to the market with some women and they helped me buy sweet oranges. From the market I went along and sold the oranges. By the time I got home in the evening, I had made one shilling and ten pence. That gave me a profit of more than double the capital I had borrowed. I was able to pay back my loan and my first childhood business flourished until I decided to go into another type of business. From that day on, I never borrowed again and never lacked money even as a child. I never depended on my parents to buy my clothing. I was one of the best-dressed kids in the neighborhood. I also became a mini-bank to my family whenever they needed a small loan.

Grace Adventure Two

I decided to change businesses and started tutoring younger students when I was between the ages of twelve and thirteen. I was in Primary Four at the time. Between our house and the next one was a small parcel of space that was not being used. I cleared a portion of it where I usually sat and did my homework and helped my younger sister with her homework. Soon other children started to come around and those in my sister's class would join us. I helped them, too. Gradually, they began to address me like a real teacher. They called me *"Sir"* as they would their schoolteachers. I was teaching English and arithmetic every afternoon after school. My sister was in Primary Two at the time. As time progressed, many more children joined us and their school grades began to improve dramatically. Their parents started calling me *Obele Teacher* meaning *small teacher*. Some of their parents began to buy me gifts; others would give me money. Their parents pointed to me as an example to their children.

At the end of the term, not one of the students that came regularly to my classes failed. Parents came to thank my mother and brought her gifts. Even wealthier families began to invite me to visit with their children in their homes. Many advised me to stop selling oranges during the holidays and asked me to concentrate on my tutoring. Some offered to pay me. I was encouraged by the support I received from both parents and pupils and especially from my older sister, who offered helpful tips, and assisted me with my own homework.

Holiday Classes

By the next holiday period, my younger sister's class had doubled in size and other children both in the lower and higher classes came to me as well. I was overwhelmed. The space was too small to contain the new group. I was not prepared for Primary Three students, and I did not have any time for myself to go out and play. However, I was able to manage each problem as they arose. I began to teach Primaries One, Two and Three. My group went from five to eleven pupils, with just one pupil in Primary Three at the beginning of the holiday classes. Two more pupils joined Primary Three and a few pupils attended the other two classes. At the end of the holiday classes and before the next term began, my income was ten shillings and that was a ton of money for me in such a short period of time. From then on the classes grew exponentially during the subsequent terms until I was teaching my own classmates.

Soon parents with pupils in higher classes than I, whose children were not doing well, began to bring them to my classes. Sometimes this meant they were just trying to get rid of them from idleness at home, so they would be engaged in some meaningful playtime activity during the evening and holiday sessions. I developed very quickly and learned a lot about myself. While preparing for those classes, I was also preparing for my future as well.

Even after I graduated from the primary school, I continued to teach those classes. I began to hire older boys and began paying them wages to teach. Even though I was young and a small boy, I was respected by all who knew me because of the grace of God that people saw in me. Parents called me *teacher*, my pupils addressed me as *Sir*, and my own parents respected me because of the grace and wisdom God had given me. Of course, I was also helping them by being financially independent from an early age.

Why the Stories

You may be asking, "Why mention these stories and how do these fairy tales show the grace of God? What is the importance of them?" God's grace is dispensed in little, seemingly inconsequential things like those shared in these stories. You do not have to win a million dollar lottery to experience and feel the grace of God. You do not have to be married to a prince like Kate Middleton or become the President of the United States like Barrack Obama to feel the blessed grace that God has showered on you from childhood.

Look back upon your own life and see the little graces you have received that helped you become who you are right now. You only need to pause and count all your blessings including: life, health, family, food, water, safety, work, education and other opportunities that you had or now have. Look around you at the many others who are dying, looking for a break, suffering horrific physical and emotional pain or have suddenly found they are homeless.

With just a few simple examples, you can look into your own life and history and see how much of the grace of God you have enjoyed over the years. While they may appear small releases within seemingly insignificant stories, each one added together with all the others has made you who you are today. Now you should be able to see the bigger blessings, the bigger picture of the grace of God in your own life. If you did an honest assessment of your life, you will agree with me that God has been generous with His grace in your life regardless of where you stand right now.

The grace of God is not only in the good things and blessings you received, but is even more evident when you consider the adversities, trials, problems, afflictions, troubles, sicknesses, accidents, and other woes that you have faced, endured, and overcome through the grace of God. The fact that you are alive today is a testimony that you are receiving the grace of God. The fact that you went to bed last night and woke up this morning while thousands of people around the world also went to bed but died in their sleep is a great testimony to God's saving grace for you. The joy that you travelled by air, land or sea and came back safely while many others lost their lives in plane crashes or some other tragedy, should remind you that you are enjoying His Divine grace.

Think of how many people who have died through car accidents, wars, train crashes, famine, and starvation. Visit a hospital near you and see for yourself what other people are going through; even innocent children are not spared. What about those people who are still languishing in jails all around the globe? How about the millions who do not have a job or reliable sources of income? Nobody is perfect and certainly no one is complete. But when you put these things together, you will begin to see what you have received, and that all you have achieved has not been accomplished by your own strength.

A song writer expressed himself so beautifully in his song, *Count Your Many Blessings name them one by one.*

This is truly the application of what we read in this passage, "Rejoice in the Lord always. I will say it again: Rejoice! Let your gentleness be evident to all. The Lord is near" (Philippians 4:4-5 NIV). Regardless of what life throws at you, remember all the good and rejoice because better days are ahead.

An angel said to Zechariah, the prophet: "This is the word of God to Zerubbabel: Not by might nor by power, but by My Spirit says the Lord of host. 'Who are you O great mountain? Before Zerubbabel you shall become plain. And he shall bring forth the capstone with shouts of Grace, grace to it'." (Zechariah 4:6-7)

This message was not to Zechariah alone because all of us face moments of crisis at one time or another. However, regardless of the mountain you are facing, you have been allotted sufficient grace to go through it. The burden gets lighter when you realize that there is grace for the particular situation you are going through. God says, "My grace is sufficient for you. For my strength is made perfect in weakness" (2 Corinthians 12:9). If the grace that is allotted to you is not sufficient for a given situation, then God by His wisdom will make a way of escape thus removing you from the situation or He will add more grace to carry you through to His desired outcome. "There has no temptation taken you but such as is common to man: but God is faithful who will not suffer you to be tempted above that you are able; but will with the temptation also make a way of escape, that you may be able to bear it" (1 Corinthians10:13).

Grace for Every Situation

There is grace for every situation under the sun; grace to rise from sleep in the morning and grace to go to sleep at night. There is grace to go through the day safely, grace for every hour, minute, and second. There is grace for driving (driving grace). There is grace for you for the particular work, sport, and business in which you are engaged. The fact that you are still engaged in that activity is a testimony of God's grace regardless of whether you are succeeding or not. There is grace for success and grace to go through failure. There is grace for all kinds of situations. I will give you one simple example that has worked for me over the years. I call it the Driving Grace.

Journey Mercy and Traveling Grace

Since I became a licensed vehicle driver, I have witnessed tremendous releases of grace on the road. I first noticed this blessing in Nigeria in the 1980's. Because of bad road conditions and insufficient road network systems, drivers and passengers spent hours on the road for a journey that should normally take just a few minutes. It was notoriously called a traffic jam. Many times at the point of the bottleneck, there was no apparent cause for such delays. Consequently drivers drove left, right, on the shoulders, even in opposite directions to beat the holdup and get to their destination on time. But, in doing so, they blocked traffic in all directions and there would be a standstill sometimes until midnight. This was almost a daily occurrence in those days.

One day stuck on a bridge after being trapped in the car for hours, I began to pray for God to open the road so I could go through. Shortly after I said the prayer, God surprised me with an answer to my prayer. Our lane began to move. When I made it passed the bottleneck the road closed again. I did not notice it immediately until I looked in my rearview mirror and discovered that the road behind me was empty. This happened quite often and with confidence, I started to pray for travelling grace even before I left home.

I have been driving for more than thirty years and have almost a perfect, accident-free record. Yet those who take a ride in my car consider me a risky driver. Some carry their hearts on their sleeves until we arrive at our destination. One woman was so uncomfortable that she asked if I was licensed to drive in Canada.

When I told her that I was first licensed in the U.S. and had never had an accident, she commented, "It is hard to believe that you never have had an accident, given the way you drive."

Then I told her that I have angelic protection when I drive, and she said, "You must be overworking them."

Driving grace and other forms of grace are a reality. I have been practicing and praying this special kind of prayer for many years now and it has never failed me. Usually during my night and morning devotion, I would add this prayer.

"Dear Lord, please dispatch your angels ahead of me to cleanse and clear my ways of all accident causing spirits, death causing spirits, all robbery causing spirits, and all breakdown causing spirits. Although the police are doing a great work of protecting us, please also remove them and the ticketing masters from my path. As you take my car and me from the parking space, also bring us back safely. My car shall not sleep outside without my express approval, in Jesus' name. Amen."

I can attest to the fact that driving grace does work. This is one of the many graces that I consciously enjoy on a daily basis. Since I have been driving, I have hardly ever had the police stop me or even issue me a single driving ticket. It is hard to believe but it is true. You, too, can think of the graces you have been enjoying on a daily basis, or you can join our grace-club where we pray for people to enter into particular Divine graces for what they ask.

Chapter 5

The Grace-Driven Life

*T*he grace-driven life is the life that is dependent on the grace of God; one that recognizes all that we are, all that we have, and all that we will ever be is dependent upon the grace of the Creator of the universe. Men tend to forget that there is one Higher Power above them for blessings, but there are also powers out there that bring harm and steal blessings. Many live their lives as if they owned this world or as if they made themselves and are accountable to no one. This is not true. Experience has shown that life does not always turn out the way we planned it. That alone should prove that we are never totally in control of our journey through this life. Therefore, we ought to humble ourselves and seek grace and guidance from the One and only true living God who controls our destinies.

The Purpose of Life

The grace-driven life is a life of purpose. There is a purpose for every one of us here on earth. No one is here by accident. There is a definite plan and purpose for you and me, and there is a definite grace for every purpose that God has put in each of us. Sometimes, grace may not be released in full if we are not living or working according to the purpose He has for us. The purpose of God is meant to give meaning and focus to our lives. The purpose of God is His will for our lives. If we are not living according to the will and purpose for our lives, then the full extent of our grace is not released. When we do not have the full measure of the grace of God, we are unproductive in our endeavors and unfulfilled in our lives.

Those of us who discover our purpose and destiny early in life enjoy a greater degree of satisfaction in whatever activity we are engaged. However, it is never too late for those of us who are just now discovering our purpose. The full measure of the grace of God is still there and available. For those who are yet to make this discovery, ask God for revelation, because His purpose comes with His grace to accomplish it.

Goal-Directed Life

A grace-driven life is a goal-directed life. The purpose of grace is to accomplish our God-given goals. There are different types of grace and each of them is given for a goal-directed purpose in the process of achieving our destiny. Grace is released according to need. It is not usually released when there is no need for it. If we are truly engaged in our divine or natural calling, grace is naturally released for that situation. Most of us go through life hurting and aching because we are out of touch with the will of God or do not know how to ask for grace in our circumstances and situations. Without grace life is miserable and bleak whether at work, in marriage or in any other endeavors of our existence. It is like one groping in the dark. But even if you have been walking on the dark side of life, when you suddenly discover your calling, passion or purpose, you will instantly see the light of His grace begin to shine on you and your joy and peace returns.

One thing that tells you that you are not within the parameters of the will and grace of God for your life's potential is the absence of peace and joy. When peace is gone, joy disappears also. It does not matter what your race, color of skin or the language you speak. Peace is the yardstick for knowing if you are doing the right thing. Therefore, if you lack peace in any area of your life, please pause and check your life's activities to see if you are actually doing what is best for you and society. Where there is no grace, God is absent. Where there is no God, purposes are useless and empty and the breeding ground for every kind of evil work is fertile. Grace is not the preservation of any religion. The grace of salvation is for those who come to God through Jesus Christ, irrespective of religious affiliations.

A Life of Plans

A grace-driven life is a life of purpose, and a life of purpose is a life of plans. When God gives a purpose, He also gives you the blueprint for that purpose. It is God's blueprint that you translate into a working plan for your life and for other projects. The plan is like a roadmap or a GPS to help you get to your desired destiny using the best route. Going through life is like going through a maze or thick forest. You will agree with me that it is very easy to miss your trail and go astray, or even be lost forever. Well-prepared and well-executed plans will lead to ultimate success. Without a plan, purposes are easily defeated. God's plan includes knowing Him, but that does not always mean that all who claim to know Him have discovered *His* plan for their lives. However, that is the starting point for all.

Just as there are different kinds of grace, there are also different types of plans including: family planning, education, finances, business or project plans. Every area of our lives requires a plan to be able to effectively coordinate our lives. When we have a proper plan in the different areas of our lives, we can clearly see where we need His grace to help in time of need or trouble.

David, the psalmist, was a man who had the plan of God for his life. In Psalm 46:1-3 he wrote, "God is my refuge and strength, a very present help in time of trouble. Therefore, we will not fear, though the earth be removed, though the mountains be carried into the midst of the sea; though the waters roar and be troubled, though the mountains shake with its swelling." David is speaking like a man who knew his God and was quite knowledgeable about the proximity of His grace in times of trouble or need.

It is always reassuring when we know that God is with us, that God is on our side, that we can call upon Him in any situation, and He answers. If you are in that kind of situation now, then you are living by grace. Living by grace means that you are dependent and reliant upon God at all times and in all circumstances. God's grace never disappoints.

Living by Grace is a State of Mind

Living by grace is a state of mind, a state of being, and certainly a state of trust. We have to trust God to be able to live by grace. The prophet Isaiah wrote, "You will keep him in perfect peace whose mind is stayed on you because he trusts in you" (Isaiah 26:3). Since grace is a gift from God and since we cannot see God with the naked eye, we simply must learn to trust that there is a God of grace who longs to meet our needs.

For those who are not very familiar with God, you can still trust that there is a superior, invisible Being (God) out there that has the power to help, bless and cover you with His grace. The mind works on the principle that whatever you consciously and repeatedly deposit in the mind will eventually be accepted and acted upon by your subconscious mind. The mind is one of the most important features of our being. It is the interface between the physical and the spiritual, between the natural and the supernatural, between the conscious, the subconscious and the superconscious. The mind only works on the passion or dominant thought, desire or idea that is uppermost on our minds at that time.

When Isaiah said, "You (God) will keep him in perfect peace, whose mind is stayed on You, because he trusts in You" (Isaiah 26:3), he was saying, in effect, that the dominant thought in his mind was to trust in God. That trust, he believed, would produce peace. If it could produce peace, it could also produce joy, health, healing, prosperity, deliverance, and forgiveness by the same process of trust. I have been quoting and reciting that verse more times than I can remember. It is my antidote for sleepless nights. Whenever my mind is overburdened and I can not sleep, I recite it over and over again until it becomes my dominant thought, and before I know it, I am asleep.

The Lord gives sleep to His beloved, "It is vain for you to rise up early, to sit up late, to eat the bread of sorrows, for he gives his beloved sleep" (Psalm 127:2). The grace to sleep is one of the most important graces that most people take for granted until they lose sleep for two or three days in a row. If it goes more than three days, you may have to pay the doctors and pharmacists to get it back. That is to say, nothing that we naturally enjoy and take for granted is free including air, water, land, a bumper harvest, etc. They are all paid for by His grace just as the free gift of salvation is not actually free. It was paid for by Jesus and given to us freely. So if you are still without Him as you personal Savior, you are taking His sacrifice on the cross of Calvary for granted. That is a serious *for-granted* and has a serious eternal consequence of living without grace for all eternity.

A Life of Thanksgiving

A grace-filled life is a life of thanksgiving. Those who live by grace know that it is a life of gratitude to the Divine for all the unmerited and undeserving grace and favor they have received free of charge. It is a life of acknowledgement of the many graces and mercies that God has shown to them. It is only the ignorant and the ungrateful that deny the existence of God. It is not possible to say I believe in grace and not in God. *The foolish* is what the scripture calls them in Psalm 14:1, "The fool has said in his heart, there is no God."

Thanksgiving is an attitude of praise and appreciation that is resident in a humble and grateful soul. Actually, God commands us to give thanks in all situations. "In everything give thanks: for this is the will of God in Christ Jesus concerning you" (1 Thessalonians 5:18). When you remember to thank and praise Him, He also will remember you when you call. A life of thanksgiving is always a life of love. Whatever we receive from above is given because He loves us. In the same way, we also should carry or show a heart of immense gratitude to Him who has blessed us with all spiritual blessing. "Blessed be the God and Father of our Lord Jesus Christ, who has blessed us with all spiritual blessings in heavenly places in Christ" (Ephesians 1:3). Instead of muttering and complaining, a heart of gratitude and prayer becomes more beneficial and promotes health and grace which releases us to honor God.

Life of Hope

A life driven by grace is a life of hope, and hope properly placed will never disappoint or put you to shame. When I say hope is properly placed, I mean anchoring your hope in the One who will never fail you. God is that Someone you can rely on totally, completely, absolutely, and unconditionally 24/7. He has your back! Hope is the driving and sustaining force of the universe. Without hope, our world would soon collapse under us like a pack of cards. But hope properly and actively placed in the only true living God will never disappoint us. Hope in Him gives us courage, strength, and security knowing He holds our future in His hands. Hope in Christ makes life worth living and takes the scariness out of death. It will give us assurance and peace that He will be there when we need it or when we call.

Chapter 6

The Origin of Grace

Grace is an attribute of God and it is the outward attribute. This means that it is one of those attributes of God that goes out from Him to bless and help unlike *glory*, which is inward to Him and He shares with no one. "I am the Lord: that is my name: and my glory I will not give to another; nor my praise to graven images" (Isaiah 42:8). Grace on the other hand, is given or released to bless, help, beautify, refine, honor, dignify, uplift and, among other things and bring attractiveness to the recipient. Grace is love in action. It is the embodiment of all the goodness, mercies, attributes, character, and the Divinity of God. In other words, grace originated from God and it is His prerogative to give it as He pleases. Grace is God's love personified. Grace is God reaching out to a lost world, giving part of His kind self to beautify and equip humanity for the task of tending this world.

Grace originated from the kindness of God's heart toward His creation. It is an intrinsic quality of the Divine. No other Being has the capacity to produce and give grace. It is one of those qualities that reside only with and in the

Almighty alone. Grace cannot be bought or earned. We cannot determine the measure that we "deserve." It is the prerogative of God as to who gets what, how much, how many, how often, and what time grace is released. Since no human has any input into the dispensation of grace, we should seek Him who alone determines our lot and grace in this life.

You will be doing yourself a great disservice, if out of pride or arrogance with the little you have received you begin to think that you are great or greater than the Giver. Be careful you do not begin to think you do not need Him or begin to question the existence of Him who holds your life in His hand. He holds you in His hand and it is only by His grace and mercy that you are even alive. "It is of the Lord's mercies that we are not consumed, because his compassions fail not. They are new every morning: great is your faithfulness" (Lamentations 3:22-23).

Grace brings God's loving-kindness, goodness and help to us in our time of need. Forgiveness of sin is only possible through grace and that is the major and most important work of grace. Sins that are not forgiven are like a heavy load, weight, or burden that will eventually crush the soul to death. That is why it is so needful that everyone experiences the grace of forgiveness of sin.

Grace Came from Jesus Christ

Until the coming of Jesus Christ, grace was not given as a general amnesty to the world. In fact, there was very little dispensation of grace in the world. Except for a very few people who were specifically chosen by God to perform special assignments (like Noah, Abraham, Joseph, David, Solomon and the prophets) the subject of grace

The Origin of Grace

was not discussed in the Old Testament. Grace came from Jesus Christ. He is God's best, highest, greatest, and eternal gift of grace to the world. Before the advent of Jesus, God gave the law or the Ten Commandments to Moses. The law basically set God's standard of acceptable behavior.

> *"I am the Lord your God who brought you out of the land of Egypt, out of the house of bondage. You shall have no other gods before me. You shall not make to yourselves any carved image, or any likeness of anything that is in the heaven above, or that is in the earth beneath, or that is in the waters under the earth, you shall not bow to them nor serve them.... You shall not murder. You shall not commit adultery. You shall not steal. You shall not bear false witness...You shall not covet..."* (Exodus 20:2-17)

If one sinned or failed to keep these laws religiously, they were stoned to death, punished, ostracized, or even worse they were not guaranteed eternal life. Now God is saying, "Come unto me all you who labor and are heavy laden, and I will give you rest" (Matthew 11:28). What a shift in the paradigm of God's approach to dealing with humanity. Jesus came so that we might live, have freedom, and abundant life here on earth and also in heaven. Jesus said, "The thief comes to steal, kill and to destroy, but I am come that you might have life more abundantly" (John 10:10). The grace that Jesus brings gives you peace, joy, abundant life, and hope of eternity (see 1 John 3:16). Jesus was manifested to destroy the graceless and merciless works of the devil that are evident everywhere in the world today.

In the beginning was the Word, and the Word was with God and the Word was God. And the Word became flesh and dwelt among us, and we beheld His glory, the glory of the Only Begotten of the Father, full of grace and truth. And of His fullness have we received, and grace for grace. For the law was given through Moses, but grace and truth came through Jesus Christ. (John 1:1, 14, 16-17)

Not only is Jesus God's grace personified, He is also the whole truth of God's existence, attributes, and love. Grace came in the fullness of time. "But when the fullness of the time had come, God sent forth his Son, born of a woman, born under the law, to redeem those who were under the law, that we might receive the adoption as sons. And because we are sons, God has sent forth the spirit of His Son into our hearts, crying out, Abba, Father. There, you are no longer slaves but sons, and if a son, then an heir of God through Christ" (Galatians 4:4-7).

One of the many works of grace is to grant us access to the presence of God so that He can easily receive our petitions and answer our prayers. Answer to prayer is as much the work of grace as physical beauty, physical strength, and physical skills. God's grace does not only have physical attributes, it is over and above the satisfying of our earthly and human needs and desires. It has eternal ramifications. Grace came to bridge the division between God and us, and to make His presence as real to us as our physical strength is real. God came in person to bring His grace to us so that we can identify with Him in a real personal way.

Grace came as a person with the name, Emmanuel. "Behold a virgin shall be with child and bear a Son, and they shall call His name Emmanuel" (Matthew 1:23). Emmanuel has been interpreted as *God with us*. The relationship between me and Immanuel is real and personal. Immanuel equals God with me. That is how close it can get; a one-to-one personal relationship of love. This brings a whole new dimension to the subject of grace which is beyond the scope of this book, but will give light to the aspects of our spiritual beauty, strength and charm that is even better, higher and more profitable than the physical attributes and endowments of grace.

How Grace Works

Grace works in two ways. First, it is a natural endowment that you inherited from birth and you can use it as is, improve upon it, and develop it. Secondly, it can come as a result of faithfully asking God for a particular grace, or gift and persisting until you receive it. Miracles work like that. A lot of folks think that miracles are reserved for the super-tele-evangelists. Please perish that idea. Miracles are graces released to those who ask for them. I know some great tele-evangelists who, when they were not anywhere near stardom, were as ordinary as anybody else. I have also witnessed countless numbers of miraculous releases of graces and answers to prayers both for myself and on behalf of others. Miraculous releasing of Divine Grace is, and should be, for everyone who believes.

I knew a man when I was younger that whenever he spoke a word of prayer, it was answered immediately to the amazement of all the people who witnessed the scenario. I tell you this to show you that anything is possible to him that believes. Just ask persistently until the grace is released. That is how grace works; just keep asking. "Do not fear, little flock, for it is your Father's good pleasure to give you the kingdom" (Luke 12:32). This means that it is God's good pleasure to give you everything you ask for, including having a part in His kingdom. However, God reserves the right to answer in His own way and in His own time.

Grace Works with Faith

"But without faith, it is impossible to please Him, for he that comes to God must believe that He is, and that He is the Rewarder of those who diligently seek Him" (Hebrews 11:6). This scripture makes it clear that dealing with God requires a simple child-like faith. What is child-like faith? A five-year-old child believes that Jerusalem is in Heaven, and what she learned in Sunday school she is willing to argue with her parents if they tell her otherwise. It is a simple, uncomplicated, unquestioning belief that there is a good God who is very near, and who wants to hear and help anytime, anywhere, anyhow. However, if we do not believe He exists and that He is a rewarder of those who seek Him, no amount of prayer will help. God is looking for sons and daughters—not beggars.

Grace Works with Prayer

Grace works with faith, and faith works with prayer. The simplest definition of prayer is talking to or communing with God. God is the closest friend we have. This is true for those of us who have the privilege of knowing a little about Him and believe strongly in Him. He is so close that we can talk to Him silently in our heart, on the bus, on the road while driving, in the classroom, in our bed, and even in the bathroom. He is always close. If you do not mind the "pooh," neither does He! He says, "I am with you always, even to the end of the world" (Matthew 28:20).

He likes to hear us pray and call or ask Him for grace. He understands and knows firsthand what we've been through, what we are going through, and even what we will go through later. What's more, He wants to give us that peace that surpasses understanding. He wants to give grace to alleviate our suffering. If the situation cannot be changed as fast as you would like, He wants to comfort us in the midst of our painful situation. More importantly, He wants to forgive our past and present sins, and restore fellowship with Him. He always wants to hear our prayers. "Pray without ceasing" (1 Thessalonians 5:17).

Faith and prayer working together will bring the power of God down to bear upon any situation. The only two exceptions for not getting your prayers answered that I know of are when the prayer is not according to the will of God for your life or faith is missing. These are very simple means of receiving grace from God. However, it is God's decision to answer as He pleases with "yes, no, or wait until the time is right."

To live by grace is to become a friend of God and this is not any more complicated than becoming a friend of anyone else. First, you have to like the person, then talk and hang out with him/her. As you continue to talk and hang out more and more, you become the best of friends and can share everything. This is how it works with God also. Talk to Him in your own way and in your own words. Remember He is the Master on all topics. Then talk more and more intimately with Him until He becomes your best friend. You can talk to God about any subject including subjects considered taboo, such as sex, drugs, and crime. Ask Him all the questions you want and you'll be surprised at the depth of His knowledge, and the variety of sources He will use to answer your questions.

Did you know that God has a sense of humor? You will be amazed at what you will find out as you hang out with Him and talk more intimately with Him. Do not make communication with God any more complicated than you would with your best friend. God is not judgmental. If He were, no one would be alive today on planet earth because everybody is a sinner. "For all have sinned and come short of the glory of God" (Romans 3:23). David, the psalmist, said, "If you should mark iniquities, O Lord, who shall stand? But there is forgiveness with You that You may be revered" (Psalm 130:3-4). Jesus said, "I desire mercy and not sacrifice. For I did not come to call the righteous; but sinners to repentance" (Matthew 9:13).

It stands to reason that prayer and faith in God will bring the grace of God to bear down on any circumstance or situation. There is everything to gain in living by grace and nothing to lose. Time invested in a prayer of faith is time well spent. This is because you will find the peace, joy, and favor you have been looking for and you will receive the inner strength to handle the tough issues of life.

Chapter 7

People Who Lived by Grace

*L*ife is filled with people who have lived by and still live by grace. Grace is the unmerited favor of God. Grace with God can never be earned but is received as a gift. The scripture is replete with examples of ordinary people, kings, and prophets who received grace and became great, famous, successful and renowned through the grace of God. We shall talk about a few of them.

Noah

"But Noah found grace in the eyes of the Lord" (Genesis 6:8). Noah was an ordinary citizen like any other person when God chose him to build the Ark. We do not even know whether he was a carpenter or a builder before God called him and gave him the inspiration to carry out such a monumental assignment. He had never heard of rain in all his life yet God asked him to build a huge ship though he did not understand its purpose (see Genesis 6:1-22).

This particular account is to show us grace does not require anything from us that it does not supply everything d to accomplish it. Grace is God being a Father to us. There are people who don't understand the full notion or importance of a father. Perhaps they never knew their father or they were never treated well or were victims of abuse. A father is supposed to be the pillar and foundation of any proper home. The father is the one who establishes his home. He provides and protects his family, and makes sure that the children are treated fairly and equally. He gives them assignments according to their strengths and abilities because he knows them from birth. He loves them equally regardless of their inherent weaknesses and shortcomings. A father is the strength and powerbase of the family. God, our Father, should be the foundation and pillar of our lives. He knows exactly what grace and gifts to assign because He understands us completely, even before birth. "Before I formed you in the womb I knew you; before you were born I sanctified you (set you apart), and ordained you" (Jeremiah 1:5).

Grace must be completely undeserved and unmerited to become a gift so that no one can boast. Moreover, grace comes with full provisions to accomplish a purpose. Noah received strength, wisdom and resources to do the impossible, the unthinkable, and the unimaginable. For Noah to build an ark of that magnitude was no small feat. It took more than a hundred years to build and cost hundreds of thousands of today's dollars in order to accomplish this task. At the end of all his hard work, Noah and his family received grace to live after the entire population of earth was completely annihilated. The truth and beauty of the grace of God is that regardless of how long it takes or how much it costs, you will accomplish your destiny if you live according to God's will for you.

Abraham

Abraham is another great example of an undeserving man who received grace, protection, and provision from God. He became known as a friend of God and the father of many nations; one of the world's super generals. He also was a normal, ordinary person, who received grace to achieve greatness unequalled by any other person. The story of Abraham is told in Genesis from Chapters 11-25. His real life started in Chapter 12.

> *Now the Lord said to Abram: "Get out of your country, from your kindred, and from your fathers' house, to a land that I will show you. I will make you a great nation; I will bless you and make your name great; and you shall be a blessing. I will bless those who bless you, and curse those who curse you; and in you shall all the families of the earth be blessed."* (Genesis 12: 1-3)

Has God spoken anything to you? Do you feel you are destined to do something or be somewhere else or be somebody else? Relax and God will bring it to pass. "For it is God who works in you both to will and to do of His good pleasure" (Philippians 2:13). Just as God spoke to Abraham and accomplished it, so will He perfect everything that He has spoken of or proposed for your life. Just hang in there like Abraham did.

Abraham believed so much in the grace and promises of God that he was ready and willing to do just what God asked of him, even to the point of actually killing his own son before God stopped him. Those who believe in the grace and promises of God know that no matter how long

difficult the going gets, God must keep His prom-
...braham was not the most righteous man in his day, but he received much grace to become such an icon for God. The difference is that Abraham believed God, and even when all hope was lost for him to ever have a child from his wife Sarah, he still believed. He was a man of incredible faith.

Sarah

Sarah was the first woman to receive monumental grace and probably it was because of her husband, Abraham. Sarah was about ninety years old when she delivered a baby boy, Isaac. In fact, Sarah was not big on faith. She had lost all hope of ever having a child and could not keep herself from laughing out loud when the angel told Abraham that she would conceive a child. Sarah was way past menopause and probably needed a walking stick just to support herself as she walked around. But when the grace of God hit her, she received strength to carry a baby for nine months, and even delivered the child without modern medical equipment or any well-trained, experienced, Harvard-certified gynecologists in attendance.

You too will receive strength when your hour of grace and visitation comes. Living by grace is holding on to God's love until He gives us the desire in our heart or until He visits us like He visited Sarah. Though Sarah may not have prayed or believed very much, she received grace to accomplish God's purpose for her on earth. Some of the grace you receive is not just for you alone, but so that God can use those graces to accomplish His plans and purposes on earth. You may not be big on faith, like Sarah, but you may have just enough faith to continue to pray until He visits you.

Joseph

There are very few men who received grace for extraordinary accomplishments like Joseph. Joseph was the eleventh out of the twelve children born to Jacob. He received the gift of dreaming big dreams and interpreting them. That gift got him into trouble and animosity within his family. Our grace can also be a source of affliction and trouble if not well managed. Joseph was betrayed and sold into slavery by his own brothers who were jealous of his gift and the love that his mother and father showered on Him. He was sold a couple of times, actually, before he found himself in prison, but his gift never left him because of God's promise, "The gifts and calling of God are irrevocable" (Romans 11:29).

Whatever gifts of grace we have received from God to accomplish a purpose are irrevocable as long as we are using them in accordance to His Divine will. Let me say here that God would not generally take a gift from us unless He considers us or the gift to be a threat to us or to humanity. In such cases, He might take the grace of purpose from you and also remove this grace. A gift of purpose is also a certificate of protection. Satan, Herod, Absalom, Saul, Samson, and Eli are examples of some of those who lost their gift of grace. Your gift should be a strong link to God and not to be abused with pride.

Joseph went from the prison to the palace and from the palace to becoming the Prime Minister of Egypt. He accomplished all these without fighting a battle or earning a Harvard degree. He humbly received grace, the gift of dreaming and interpreting dreams, and used this grace intentionally and appropriately for the purpose for which it was destined. That is why the scripture says, "A man's gift makes room for him and brings him before great men" (Proverbs 18:16). Joseph went on to become not only a ruler in Egypt, but he became a succor and a sustainer for his entire family, including those who sold him into slavery. This is an example of how gifts of grace should be used.

David

Like Joseph, David was at the bottom of the list of his siblings. He was the eighth of eight children born to a man named Jesse. David was so unrecognized as inconsequential that when God sent the prophet Samuel to anoint one of Jesse's sons as king, David was not even informed to come and welcome the prophet. He was left in the fields tending his father's smelly sheep. He was a poor shepherd boy, but God had already deposited His grace upon him and when the time was right, His grace spoke up. I pray that your grace will speak up for you in your time of need.

When you read the account of David starting in 1st Samuel 16 and then all of 2nd Samuel, you will discover how a man's gift can seek him out even if he is banished into the desert. Notice how grace works not by your power or your might, and certainly not by your wisdom or education, but by the Spirit of God upon your life. It will search you out, bless you, and promote you to your next level. Let us read a small portion of his account. While David was busy in the fields with the animals, God was busy preparing a kingdom for him. "And God said to Samuel, how long will you mourn for Saul, seeing I have rejected him from reigning over Israel? Fill your horn with oil and go; I am sending you to the house of Jesse, the Bethlehemite; for I have provided myself a king among his sons" (1 Samuel 16:1). This was shortly after God had rejected Saul because of his partial obedience.

When the prophet arrived and was invited to see the sons of Jesse, David was not invited. When the grace of God is upon our life, God will make a way for us even if we are not invited to our own ceremony. After the prophet inspected the seven older sons of Jesse, he did not find the man of grace that God told him about (verses 6-10). Then he asked, "Are all the young men here?" (1 Samuel 16:11a). Our grace will ask for us, even if we are omitted in the thing that concerns us most. Then Jesse said, "There is yet the youngest, he is keeping the sheep" (1 Samuel 16:11b). In other words, he is doing the dirty work. And Samuel said, "Send and bring him, for I will not sit down till he has come here" (1 Samuel 16:11c). May your grace make a way for you and bring you before kings and queens. May your grace give your oppressors sleepless nights. May your opportunities not sit down until you have inherited your due blessings. When David finally arrived, he was instantly anointed King of Israel.

The gift of receiving great grace does not mean the gift of a trouble-free life. On the contrary, the more grace we receive, the more trouble or affliction we receive. It is the comforting and sustaining aspects of grace that makes the burden of the highly gifted bearable or lighter. Some of us cannot stand or face what highly graced people face. The popular adage says, "Uneasy lays the head that wears a crown." So when we are asking God for a high and visible grace, remember also the thistle or thorn that comes with the beautiful rose flower.

David went on to become king over Israel, but at a very great cost to his way of living. His saving grace was that he relied on God the whole time, as did Joseph, Abraham and Noah. Living by grace is simply recognizing the grace we have, nurturing it, and putting it to its intended use. The fact that someone received a small grace does not mean that the person receiving a higher grace is credited more. Grace is the same. It is a means of accomplishing the purpose of God here on earth. It is the faithfulness with which we pursue and use our gifts and graces that is credited and not the gift itself.

Grace is such a powerful gift. Sometimes it is very evident in a person from childhood like the case of Jesus Christ of Nazareth. Other times, it is barely noticeable until adulthood like Barack Obama, President of the United States of America. There is still another type of grace that leads to helping those who are suffering. It is a grace that blesses other people including those working in impoverished countries of the world and those in places of conflicts. They are called aid workers, volunteers, and missionaries. Instead of enjoying grace and comfort, they are laying down their lives for others. Whatever your grace or calling, grace is what makes the difference between success and failure, and between fulfilling your destiny and not reaching your destiny.

Barack Obama

Perhaps, the example of grace that we can best relate to is the ascendency of Barack Obama to the Presidency of the United States of America. No one else in modern history best exemplifies the power of grace than his story. His story is no different than other examples we have already seen. The difference is that his story is currently in our time. Many know this story better than I, but all of us have one thing in common, we are eyewitnesses. He was born of an African father from Kenya studying in the United States, and a white American mother from Wichita, Kansas. He barely knew his father. Around age six he was taken to Indonesia and four years later he came to the United States. From his background, he did not seem like anyone special by any glint of the imagination. However, his destiny had been sealed by the grace he received from birth. No one knew him nationally, and not even a single member of his immediate family knew of his grace.

By the typical jobs he chose after graduation from the university and during his law school years, no one would document these as prerequisites to becoming President of the United States of America. However, in the fullness of time the grace and the gift of purpose made a deposit in his life. It located him, energized him, and gathered all the resources necessary to bring him to where he is today. Most people recognized him clearly as the underdog in the race to the White House in 2007. But it was not too long before his gifts began to make room for him. Both grace and favor were fully on his side.

There have been only a handful of such election campaigns in the history of America, however, none as expensive as the 2007/2008 presidential elections. As a clear underdog, his opponents were far richer and more experienced, with intimidating political and military portfolios, but in the end he won a decisive victory to become the first Black American President of the United States, the Land of Milk and Honey. As if the battles to the presidency were child's play, he was faced with the more formidable and daunting task of pulling the United States economy out of a deep depression. As long as he keeps his eyes focused on God, the Giver of grace, who has seen him through thus far, the provision in his calling will continue to be more than enough for him. "My grace is sufficient for you; for my strength is made perfect in weakness" (2 Corinthians 12:9).

Kate Middleton (Duchess of Cambridge)

Kate is the second woman in our series of examples who received noteworthy grace. From her biography, she was born into a British regular working class family. At birth there was nothing special about her except that in her destiny was invisibly written "grace to marry a prince." Then grace began to direct her path in life. There are probably tens or hundreds of people with royal ties that Prince William *could* have chosen as a bride, and Kate may not have been the only girl that the Prince dated. But the grace that Kate received stopped all others, and today she is no longer a *commoner*, as the British call anyone who is not of royal descent. She is now Her Royal Highness, The Duchess of Cambridge, a calling that very few have been able to achieve throughout history.

I believe that the Duchess would agree with me that her present position was absolutely attained by grace. Great graces such as the ones our examples received always come with a higher price. No one has ever received a great grace for major achievements that does not pay a price for it. The Apostle Paul explained it in 2 Corinthians 12:7, "And lest I should be exalted above measure through the abundance of the revelations, there was given to me a thorn in the flesh, a messenger of Satan to buffet me, lest I should be exalted above measure."

I believe every president, king and queen would agree whole-heartedly to this age long adage, "Uneasy lays the head that wears a crown." [Author unknown]. Those of us who receive lesser graces should be very thankful, for none of us can endure what these great people have endured with the type of grace they were given.

Chapter 8

Those Who Lost Their Grace

*T*here are as many examples of those who lost their grace as of those who lived by it. Let no one be deceived to think that because his grace is not as great as others that he can trifle with it. No grace or gift is greater than the other. Whether it is grace to be a president or a schoolteacher, every grace is given for a purpose. As all men are born equal, even though some are born in palaces, so all gifts and graces are given and rated equally to all men, even though some gifts shine brighter than others. Here are examples of some who lost or mishandled their gifts of grace.

Adam and Eve

The most obvious example of those who lost their grace is that of Adam and Eve. These two great people were our ancestors. They saw God face-to-face, talked with Him, walked with Him, and enjoyed His visits. God provided everything they needed to live well and live forever in a paradise. However, they lost everything, including their freedom and peace because of an act of carelessness and disobedience. Not only did they lose their grace to live in the Garden of Eden, they plunged humanity into a perpetual cycle of sin, suffering, pain, and death. They derailed God's plans and purposes for humanity because of one act of willful disobedience (see Genesis 3:1-24). The story of Adam and Eve serves to teach us how dangerous the sin of willful disobedience to God's Word can be. Thank God for this dispensation of grace. It would have been very disastrous for this generation of ours, if God had not shown His mercy at that time. May God continue to have mercy upon us!

Cain

Cain, the first born son of Adam became the first member of the second generation to lose grace. Cain murdered his brother, Abel, because of envy and hatred of his brother's gifts and grace. Because of the wickedness in Cain's heart, God cursed him and banished him from society, and he became a fugitive, a vagabond, and an outcast (see Genesis 4:8-13). Cain received the notorious title of the world's first murderer. This is a lesson for those who are not content with what they have, and for those who choose to entertain feelings of envy, jealousy, and hatred of others. These hidden sins of the heart are very destructive, and are not easily detected from looks and outward appearances.

Absalom

Absalom, King David's first son, had wealth, fame, favor, beauty, charisma, and the grace to succeed his father and become a great king. But he lost all he had and died a shameful, untimely, and unnecessary death. Even those born with a silver spoon in their mouth also fall into the trap of not valuing their gifts and graces. They also take it for granted and fail to remember that whoever they are and whatever they have been given is by grace and not by luck. Absalom thought he could hurry his way into his destiny. No one can do that! Destiny must run its natural course. Patience is a great virtue. Those who lack it pay a huge price for their impatience. In a hurry, Absalom tried to usurp his father's throne and waged war against him. In the process, he died in the battle without a wife or a child to succeed him. That is called the sin of abuse and overstepping. The story of Absalom is found in 2 Samuel 15 through 18:18.

Nebuchadnezzar

There was no greater king and as powerful in his day as King Nebuchadnezzar who reigned as King of Babylon. History has it that Nebuchadnezzar ruled the world. But Nebuchadnezzar lost that grace when his heart was lifted in pride and proclaimed himself worthy to be worshipped as a god. He refused to acknowledge the God of Heaven. Some people choose to worship their gifts more than the Giver. Others use their gifts to intimidate, cheat, harass, and kill others. Some even ascribe their gifts and graces to Satan. Whenever we use our gifts for purposes for which they were not intended, there are always conditional consequences. King Nebuchadnezzar became so powerful in his own conceit that he denied and forbade the worship of the Living God. God punished and banished him into the forest for seven years. This is my interpretation of what transpired in Daniel 4:27-33.

"O king, and this is the decree of the Most High, which is come upon my lord the king: that they shall drive you from men, and your dwelling shall be with the beasts of the field, and they shall make you to eat grass as oxen, and they shall wet you with the dew of heaven, and seven times shall pass over you, till you know that the Most High rules in the kingdom of men, and gives it to whomsoever he chooses. In as much as the command was given to leave the stump and roots of the tree, your kingdom shall be assured to you, after you come to know that Heaven rules. Therefore, O king, let my counsel be acceptable to you; break off your sins by righteousness, and your iniquity by showing mercy. Perhaps, there may be a lengthening of your prosperity."

All this came upon King Nebuchadnezzar and at the end of twelve months; he was walking about the royal palace of Babylon saying, "Is not this great Babylon that I have built for a royal dwelling by my mighty power and for the honor of my majesty?"

While the words were still in the king's mouth, a voice came from heaven saying, "King Nebuchadnezzar, to you it is spoken, 'The kingdom is departed from you!' And they shall drive you from men, and your dwelling shall be with beasts of the field. They shall make you eat grass as oxen; and seven times shall pass over you, until you know that the Most High rules in the kingdom of men, and gives it to whomsoever He chooses."

That very hour the word was fulfilled concerning King Nebuchadnezzar. He was driven from men and ate grass like an ox. His body was wet with the dew of heaven until his hair had grown like eagle's feathers and his nails like bird's claws. The good thing about King Nebuchadnezzar was that he repented of his sins of pride and arrogance, and acknowledged the God of Heaven, the Giver of power and grace. God restored Him back to his throne and gave him back his kingdom. God is a forgiving God. Carefully read what Nebuchadnezzar said in Daniel 4:34-37 at the end of his time of insanity.

> *At the end of the time I, Nebuchadnezzar, lifted up my eyes to heaven, and my understanding returned to me; and I blessed the Most High and praised and honored Him who lives forever. His dominion is an everlasting dominion, and his kingdom is from generation to generation. All the inhabitants of the earth are reputed as nothing. He does according to His will in the army of heaven and among the inhabitants of the earth. No one can restrain His Hand or say to Him, "What have you done?" At the same time, my reason returned to me, and for the glory of my kingdom, my honour and splendor returned to me. My counselors and nobles resorted to me, I was restored to my kingdom, and excellent majesty was added to me. Now I, Nebuchadnezzar, praise and extol and honor the King of heaven, all of whose work are truth and justice. And those who walk in pride He is able to abase.*

This passage is included to show that no one is untouchable and no one is above God. When we try to ascribe or arrogate to ourselves the glory and honor due God, He will resist it. God does not share His glory with another nor take lightly the sin of pride. The scripture says, "Pride goes before destruction and a haughty spirit before a fall"

(Proverbs 16:18). We should all possess a heart of humility when we realize that God has given us a great gift.

Judas Iscariot

Judas Iscariot was a man called by Jesus, Himself, and destined to become one of the Twelve Apostles, whose fall from grace was inexcusable and unexplainable. He saw Jesus face-to-face, ate with Him, slept in the same room with Him, and witnessed His great teachings. He saw the miracles, His Divine power, and heard Peter proclaim that Jesus was the Son of God. Judas saw Jesus walk on the water, turn water into wine, and raise Lazarus from the dead. Yet, because of his love of money, he betrayed his Savior; the One and Only Person who could help him overcome his lust. Judas knowingly betrayed the One who came to save him and who gave His place to a thief who was already on his way to hell. How could anyone who lived so close to Jesus go to hell? However, as wicked as Judas was, if he had humbled himself and repented and asked for forgiveness, I believe with all of my heart that Jesus would have forgiven him. Jesus came to seek and to save those who were, and are still, lost in sin (see Matthew 18:11).

When people try to live entirely by their own strength and wisdom, they make many mistakes. Had Judas relied on Jesus, just like the other disciples, he would not have lost his grace and his place in the Kingdom of God. I encourage you, as you are reading these words, to put your faith and your life in God's hands and know that living by grace will be the safest way to go. Almost every one of us has, at one time or another betrayed the Master in some way. This book is to help everyone know that there is forgiveness and pardon in the grace of God if we but humble ourselves, repent, and ask for mercy.

Why Grace Is Not Working for Some

The above examples are about those who received extraordinary grace of purpose to lead, or to do some extraordinary things. You may be asking about your ordinary, humble self, "What grace did I receive, and why is my grace not working for me?" Every one of us is given grace according to the measure of faith that we also receive. Some receive grace to be servants, helpers, to assist kings, and presidents to achieve their purposes. Others receive grace to be doctors, soldiers, architects, farmers, and teachers. In the eyes of the Giver of grace, all gifts are equal, all gifts are related, and all gifts are necessary to construct the human community that God has sent us to build here on earth.

Like our earthly buildings, there are different components or structures that make up the building. Some are visible and external like the roof, paint, doors, and windows. Others are like the foundation and rods that are invisibly buried many feet below the ground and covered with dirt and cement. Their roles are very crucial in the stability of the structure. Therefore, let no man despise his gifts or grace. Otherwise, you will never be fulfilled or be truly happy in anything you do, no matter how much money you make. Money should not be the only driving force in pursuing our goal or calling in life. Our gifts and package of grace will open doors and opportunities for us. It will help to attract the kinds of people and resources that we will need to accomplish our destiny.

However, if we reject our gifts and graces and envy those of another, we are likely to have a hard time in life because we are turning away from the very foundations of our existence. We are, in fact, telling the Giver of all grace that He was wrong in giving us the kind of gifts we received. "Look, God, You are wrong. I know better. I should have received what the other person got; he doesn't deserve it. I am the right one for this or that grace." You may be dead wrong about yourself and the other person. You have become deluded and wise in your own conceit. In such a situation, your grace will not work for you. This scenario is the root of envy and evil works and is not the fulfillment of your life.

The scripture says, "But godliness with contentment is great gain" (1Timothy 6:6). Contentment is a great virtue. If you want to be happy, peaceful, fulfilled, and truly successful in this life, you must be truly content with whoever you are. I have seen poor and unlovely people who are happy and contented with the little they have and I praise God for them. I have also seen rich, beautiful or handsome people who are wretched and miserable. We hear and read every now and then of wealthy millionaires who commit suicide. Godliness with contentment is very profitable to all.

God has given us unfettered access to His presence through Jesus Christ to bring our requests, frustrations, anxieties, needs, problems, desires, ambitions, and prayers to Him. He admonishes us in the scripture, "Be anxious for nothing, but in everything by prayer and supplication, with thanksgiving, let your request be made known unto God; and the peace of God that passes all understanding, will guard your hearts and mind through Jesus Christ" (Philippians 4:4).

Grace will work for you whether you know of its existence or not because, to a large extent, the operations of the gifts of grace are more spiritual than physical. They are coded in your "spiritual DNA" which carries your spiritual genetic information. There is a spiritual command center for everybody, where all the operations of your life are commanded and controlled. The scripture gives us some insight into the operations of this command and control center.

> *Now concerning spiritual gifts, brethren, I would not have you ignorant...Now, there are diversities of gifts, but the same Spirit. There are differences of administration, but the same Lord. And there are diversities of operations, but it is the same Lord that worketh all in all. But the manifestation of the Spirit is given to each one for the profit of all (with all). For to one is given by the Spirit the word of wisdom; to another the word of knowledge by the same Spirit; to another faith by the same Spirit; to another gifts of healing by the same Spirit; to another the working of miracles; to another prophesy; to another discerning of spirits; to another diverse kind of tongues; to another the interpretation of tongues. But one and the same Spirit works all these things, distributing to each one individually as He wills. And God has set in the church, first apostles, secondly prophets, thirdly teachers, after that miracle (workers), then gifts of healings, helps governments....* (1 Corinthians 12:1-11, 28)

The core spiritual gifts are not the subject of this book, though people should be content with what they have and try to improve them. The God that gives a high IQ is the one that gives a low IQ for the achievement of His set of purposes. Both spiritual and natural (or physical) gifts come from the same source. That is why the scripture commands us to guard our hearts with all diligence because from there flows all the issues and forces of life. A portion or section of the command and control center is in your mind and the other is in the spirit or is spiritual. While all may not be able to control what happens in the celestial, you can control what happens in your mind. The mind controls and is the gateway into the spiritual. We shall delve into the subject of the mind later in this book.

Living in the Miraculous

Living by grace is living in the miraculous. It means expecting something new to happen to you every day. They might not be earth-shaking events all the time, but there is always new hope, new expectations, new joys, new levels of peace, new prayers answered, new self-discovery, new levels of growth and relationship with God, new love, new challenges conquered, new battles won, new obstacles overcome, new breakthroughs, and of course new souls won into the kingdom. They might also include some great achievements, new and spectacular attainments, miraculous healings, Divine interventions, Divine provisions and releases, angelic visitations, new promotions, great milestones achieved, finding the right life partner or finding the right job or business.

Living in the miraculous might even include starting all over again, embarking on new adventures, overcoming sicknesses and disease, growing old gracefully with joy and without fear, rediscovering yourself with new strengths, and overcoming old weaknesses through prayer and the power of God. Living in the miraculous includes deliverance from all kinds of home and road accidents, fire, flood, stray bullets, earthquakes, tsunamis, and all natural and man-made disasters that are commonplace in the world today. Living in the miraculous is living one day at a time, but with a great assurance that you have a very big God who is always on your side. No matter what, your life is safe and secure in His hand.

When we hear of miracles, we think only of dead men rising, the lame walking, the blind seeing, etc. Those are definitely miracles! Have you ever thought that there is no greater miracle than winning a soul to Christ and into the Kingdom of God? In case you are in need of a big miracle, God is still in the business of giving miraculous graces. He is still making the infertile or expectant mother to bear healthy children. He is still healing cancers, diabetes, high blood pressure, and all the big killer diseases. God has not changed. He is still the same, and He will do it for you if you ask and believe in His power. You may be thinking, my time is past and my miracles are over. Read what the Lord said in Isaiah 40:27-31.

> *Why do you say, O Jacob, and speak, O Israel: "My way is hidden from the LORD, and my just claim is passed over by my God"? Have you not known? Have you not heard? The everlasting God, the LORD, The Creator of the ends of the earth, neither faints nor is weary. His understanding is unsearchable. He gives power to the weak, and to those who have no might He increases strength. Even the youth shall faint and be weary, and the young men shall utterly fall, but those who wait on the LORD*

Shall renew their strength; they shall mount up with wings like eagles, they shall run and not be weary, they shall walk and not faint.

God is still working miracles in the lives of those who believe and ask. Your own grace may be just around the corner. Grace for the impossible never ceases.

Chapter 9

Fear, Anxiety and Worry

*F*ear, worry and anxiety are man's most dangerous, secret enemies. Anxiety breeds worry and worry leads to fear. Fear has such devastating and dangerous consequences to health, the mind, and to your spirit. Up until now, medical science and psychology have not yet been able to find a cure for it. But Jesus gave us the cure more than 2,000 years ago and He called it faith. Fear is lack of or the absence of faith. Fear is a state of mind. Faith also is a state of mind. Think of your mind as a switch which you can flip on and off at will. Your light switch is an example of how fickle and powerful the mind is. You flip it on and off, but each time with a different result. When you flip it to the *ON* position, the light comes on and when in the *OFF* position, the light goes off and darkness follows. So is your mind.

You can flip it to faith or to fear, whether inadvertently or not, the faith-light will come on or go off depending in which position the mind-switch is pointing. Your mind is the switchboard and you can control it anyway you like. You are as strong or as weak as you think, but the reality is in your pattern of thinking. For example, thoughts of doubt, indecision, and unbelief will gel to become fear. Indecision is the seed of uncertainty, and uncertainty is a nesting ground for worry, fear, and anxiety. Wherever these three are found fear is likely to exist. Even when life is uncertain, you can have comfort in the wisdom and power of the All-Knowing God to make things clear or to protect and cover you.

Fear has been described as **F**alse **E**vidence **A**ppearing **R**eal. There is a lot of truth in this acronym.

F- False
E- Evidence
A- Appearing
R- Real

Fear should have no place in our lives. Give it no room. Fear may be behind many emotional and spiritual problems that cannot be detected under the microscope. Fear will bring the heart into bondage and make the whole body weak, sick, powerless to proceed, fight, or even think properly. Fear is always counter-productive to faith. Living by grace will not be possible if you are living in fear. The question then becomes which would you choose fear or faith? The life of fear is a sickly and sub-standard life. But the life of faith is a strong, vibrant and happy one.

You rob yourself of the joy of living when you allow yourself to be conquered by fear, "...fear has torment" (1 John 4:18). You can be tormented by the fear of sickness, failure, poverty, criticism, people, death or any other thing that you allow to master your mind. But the good news is you can be free from the spirit of fear. "For God has not given us the spirit of fear, but of power and of love and of a sound mind" (2 Timothy1:7). You can be free of fear by the operation of the spirit of grace. When you understand and work in the spirit of grace, the spirit of fear, or anything else for that matter, can not easily intimidate you.

As mentioned earlier on, the antidote to fear is faith. To overcome fear you must take action. Act on the Word of God. Take action against the things that make you afraid. Activate your prayer life. Rise up and do things differently. Changing thought patterns is a good place to start; think positively and act courageously. Come out of your shell and take a step of faith. Fear can be conquered with prayer. There is always grace for those who believe and take positive action. Fear will rob us of the joy and blessings of living by grace. I am not writing as one who has conquered all my fears, but as one who is progressively winning the battle against this wicked enemy of man. Stand up against those things that are most bothersome.

Managing Fear

Fear does not always have to have a negative impact on us. Fear can be turned into strength and become a source of motivation. Fear can be turned into power because there is an incredible hidden power in fear. Fear has a positive side to it. You can overcome your fear as most of what we fear never comes true. It is false evidence, scenarios or perceptions that appear real as though it will happen. Turn those fears into a drive that will push you to do incredible things. Instead of allowing fear to take control, the fear must be controlled. When fear is in the driver's seat, the car goes into reverse gear or reverse mode. However, when you get back into the driver's seat success and great achievements will be easily accomplished. After all, who

Fear, Anxiety and Worry

owns the car? The car is your mind and Mr. Fear is an unwanted passenger. Would anyone allow an unwanted, crazy rider to stay in the car?

Fear is always a crazy driver whenever he is in the driver's seat. Why don't you stand up to Mr. Fear and say, "Hey, man, get right out of this car because this is my car and I am tired of giving you a free ride! I am in charge of this car by Divine mandate. I no longer need your services." Then wait and see how fast and how much you can accomplish in a short time. Fear is not from God, and we must not allow it to ruin our lives. The antidote to fear is action. Positive action will break the backbone of the spirit of fear in your life.

A friend of mine once told me that she used to be afraid of the night or darkness. One night she came home after dark to an empty house. In the height of her fear and worry, she spontaneously started singing and praising God out loud. When she was tired of singing, she started to talk out loud to herself, and banging her fist on the table as if teaching someone. She was doing exactly that! She was teaching Mr. Fear a lesson. She said her fear left her as she repeated the action over and over many times. That night she overcame her fear of the dark. She was able to sleep alone that night and many nights afterwards. Even now when she is walking alone and uneasiness creeps in, she sings to God and talks out loud to herself.

Confidence is built when a fear is overcome. There is a built-in power that is encapsulated within each fear. Within our fear is what we really want or desire. It's like a kernel and the shell must break to reach the nut inside. Your joy, peace, freedom, success, and fulfillment are hidden within your fear. You must break that nut and spill the cycle of fear if you are to achieve your dreams and goals. The job of the spirit of fear is to stop you from using or unleashing your full potential. That is the work of the devil. We are an incredible machine; capable of doing anything or reaching any height, but we are also very fearful to adventure into the unknown. I am included in this statement. Think of how many things you could have achieved had you not been afraid of one thing or another.

It is said that less than 5% of all people use their full potential. Fear is the stopper designed to make us impotent and less effective. That is why it repeatedly says in the Old and New Testaments, "Fear not" and "Do not be afraid." These are the first words that the angel, the Spirit of God, or Jesus spoke to those who encountered Him.

Fear Not

There is hardly any book of the Bible in which God has not left us this message. Below are some examples. These passages underscore the great importance that the Spirit of God attaches to the evil activities of the wicked spirit. Read what God has to say to His people about fear. They are encouraging and comforting. (I have added the underlining to emphasis my point.)

Genesis 15:1 - *After these things the word of the LORD came unto Abram in a vision, saying, "Fear not, Abram. I am thy shield, and thy exceeding great reward."*

Genesis 21:17 - *And God heard the voice of the lad; and the angel of God called to Hagar out of heaven, and said unto her, "What aileth thee,*

Hagar? *Fear not*, for God hath heard the voice of the lad where he is."

Genesis 26:24 - And the LORD appeared unto him the same night, and said, "I am the God of Abraham thy father; *fear not*, for I am with thee, and will bless thee, and multiply thy seed for my servant Abraham's sake."

Genesis 46:3 - And he said, "I am God, the God of thy father; *fear not* to go down into Egypt; for I will there make of thee a great nation."

Exodus 20:20 - And Moses said unto the people, "*Fear not*: for God is come to prove you, and that his fear may be before your faces, that ye sin not."

Deuteronomy 1:21 - "Behold, the LORD thy God hath set the land before thee; go up and possess it, as the LORD God of thy fathers hath said unto thee; *fear not*, neither be discouraged."

Deuteronomy 20:3 - And shall say unto them, "Hear, O Israel, ye approach this day unto battle against your enemies; let not your hearts faint, *fear not*, and do not tremble, neither be ye terrified because of them."

Deuteronomy 31:6 - "Be strong and of a good courage, *fear not*, nor be afraid of them; for the LORD thy God, He it is that doth go with thee; He will not fail thee, nor forsake thee."

Deuteronomy 31:8 - *"And the LORD, He it is that doth go before thee; He will be with thee, He will not fail thee, neither forsake thee; <u>fear not</u>, neither be dismayed."*

Joshua 8:1 - *And the LORD said unto Joshua, "<u>Fear not</u>, neither be thou dismayed; take all the people of war with thee, and arise, go up to Ai; see, I have given into thy hand the king of Ai, and his people, and his city, and his land."*

Joshua 10:25 - *And Joshua said unto them, "<u>Fear not</u>, nor be dismayed, be strong and of good courage; for thus shall the LORD do to all your enemies against whom ye fight."*

Judges 6:10 - *And I said unto you, "I am the LORD your God; <u>fear not</u> the gods of the Amorites, in whose land ye dwell; but ye have not obeyed my voice."*

Ruth 3:11 - *"And now, my daughter, <u>fear not</u>; I will do to thee all that thou requirest; for all the city of my people doth know that thou art a virtuous woman."*

I Kings 17:13 - *And Elijah said unto her, "<u>Fear not</u>; go and do as thou hast said: but make me thereof a little cake first, and bring it unto me, and after, make for thee and for thy son."*

II Kings 6:16 - *And he answered, "<u>Fear not</u>: for they that be with us are more than they that be with them."*

I Chronicles 28:20 - *And David said to Solomon, his son, "Be strong and of good courage, and do it; <u>fear not</u>, nor be dismayed; for the LORD God, even my God, will be with thee; He will not fail thee, nor forsake thee, until thou hast finished all the work for the service of the house of the LORD."*

II Chronicles 20:17 - *"Ye shall not need to fight in this battle; set yourselves, stand ye still, and see the salvation of the LORD with you, O Judah and Jerusalem; <u>fear not</u>, nor be dismayed; tomorrow go out against them: for the LORD will be with you."*

Isaiah 35:4 - *Say to them that are of a fearful heart, "Be strong, <u>fear not</u>; behold, your God will come with vengeance, even God with a recompense; he will come and save you."*

Isaiah 41:13-14 - *"For I the LORD thy God will hold thy right hand, saying unto thee, <u>Fear not</u>; I will help thee. <u>Fear not</u>, thou worm, Jacob, and ye men of Israel; I will help thee, saith the LORD, and thy redeemer, the Holy One of Israel."*

Isaiah 43:1 - *But now thus saith the LORD that created thee, "O Jacob, and He that formed thee, O Israel, <u>Fear not</u>; for I have redeemed thee, I have called thee by thy name; thou art mine."*

Isaiah 43:5 - "_Fear not_; for I am with thee; I will bring thy seed from the east, and gather thee from the west."

Isaiah 44:2 - Thus saith the LORD that made thee, and formed thee from the womb, which will help thee; "_Fear not_, O Jacob, my servant; and thou, Jesurun, whom I have chosen."

Isaiah 54:4 - "F_ear not_; for thou shalt not be ashamed; neither be thou confounded; for thou shalt not be put to shame: for thou shalt forget the shame of thy youth, and shalt not remember the reproach of thy widowhood any more."

Jeremiah 46:27 - "But _fear not_ thou, O my servant Jacob, and be not dismayed, O Israel; for, behold, I will save thee from afar off, and thy seed from the land of their captivity; and Jacob shall return, and be in rest and at ease, and none shall make him afraid."

Daniel 10:12 - Then said He unto me, "_Fear not_, Daniel; for from the first day that thou didst set thine heart to understand, and to chasten thyself before thy God, thy words were heard, and I am come for thy words."

Daniel 10:19 -And said, "O man greatly beloved, _fear not_; peace be unto thee, be strong, yea, be strong." And when He had spoken unto me, I was strengthened, and said, "Let my Lord speak; for thou hast strengthened me."

Fear, Anxiety and Worry

Joel 2:21 - "*Fear not*, O land; be glad and rejoice; for the LORD will do great things."

Zechariah 8:13 - "And it shall come to pass, that as ye were a curse among the heathen, O house of Judah, and house of Israel; so will I save you, and ye shall be a blessing; *fear not*, but let your hands be strong."

Matthew 1:20 - But while he thought on these things, behold, the angel of the Lord appeared unto him in a dream, saying, "Joseph, thou son of David, *fear not* to take unto thee Mary thy wife; for that which is conceived in her is of the Holy Ghost."

Matthew 10:28 - "And *fear not* them which kill the body, but are not able to kill the soul; but rather fear Him which is able to destroy both soul and body in hell."

Luke 1:13 - But the angel said unto him, "*Fear not*, Zacharias; for thy prayer is heard; and thy wife Elisabeth shall bear thee a son, and thou shalt call his name John."

Luke 2:10 - And the angel said unto them, "*Fear not*; for, behold, I bring you good tidings of great joy, which shall be to all people."

Luke 5:10 - And so was also James, and John, the sons of Zebedee, which were partners with Simon; And Jesus said unto Simon, "*Fear not*; from henceforth thou shalt catch men."

Luke 8:50 - *But when Jesus heard it, he answered him, saying, "<u>Fear not</u>; believe only, and she shall be made whole."*

Luke 12:7 - *"But even the very hairs of your head are all numbered. <u>Fear not</u> therefore; ye are of more value than many sparrows."*

Luke 12:32 - *"<u>Fear not</u>, little flock; for it is your Father's good pleasure to give you the kingdom."*

John 12:15 - *"<u>Fear not</u>, daughter of Zion; behold, thy King cometh, sitting on an ass's colt."*

Acts 27:24 - *Saying, "<u>Fear not</u>, Paul; thou must be brought before Caesar; and, lo, God hath given thee all them that sail with thee."*

Revelation 1:17 - *And when I saw him, I fell at his feet as dead. And he laid his right hand upon me, saying unto me, "<u>Fear not</u>; I am the first and the last."*

What Is the Source of Fear?

What is the source of fear? Why do we feel fear at all? Have you ever taken the time to find out what you are really afraid of and why? When and how did the fear start? If you cannot face it, you will never be able to overcome it. If you are uncertain, seek out adequate help to deal with it once and for all. These are very pertinent questions you have to answer before you can rid yourself of debilitating fears.

Fear is a spirit that lives and works within your emotions. It can paralyze the intellect, destroy the will, cancel ambition, disgrace a man, and stifle emotions. Fear can also supplant reason, cause suspicion, anger and frustration. It has ruined marriages, destroyed trust, separated friends and families, failed pupils in exams, and denied people of joy, peace, love and friendship. Fear can make a man impotent and a woman sterile. Fear brings false accusations and can cause you to tell lies. In fact, every lie is the result of fear of something, such as a punishment or of someone. The list of reasons is endless.

God gave mankind those verses because He knew our weaknesses and vulnerability. He hates fear with a passion, and wants us to destroy it when and where it is found. This writer has been involved in helping people deal with and destroy the spirit of fear through spiritual counseling and prayer for many years. "For God has not given us the spirit of fear but of power, and of love and of a sound mind" (2 Timothy 1:7).

The good news is that fear can be overcome. Fear can be mastered, and fear can be defeated. No matter what type of fear you may have, there is help and there is deliverance.

Types of Fear

There are many different types of fears. People fear everything from earthworms to ordinary darkness. But some very prominent of our normal and abnormal fears fall under these examples which, include, but are not limited to:

Fear of God
Fear of man or people
Fear of criticism

Fear of death and old age
Fear of sickness or ill health
Fear of public speaking
Fear of failure
Fear of poverty
Fear of rejection
Fear of the unknown
Fear of the future
Fear of height and so on

These types of fear are common with man, but rarely materialize unless they become an obsession. God does not want us to live under their crippling effects.

Anxiety

Anxiety is an unnecessary concern over something of which you do not have control. It is an apprehension that robs the mind of the ability to function productively and at full capacity. Anxiety is a distress of the soul or a distraction. It makes the body nervous, fretful and impatient, and destabilizes the whole nervous system. To a large extent anxiety does not produce any good fruit. Even when people are anxious for a good reason, they have been known to make mistakes over things they can control because they were so anxious to get it over with. Good students have been known to fail exams just because they were anxious during the exam. They became careless and made many simple mistakes. Anxiety does not do any good and should be avoided at all cost. Anxiety works well with worry, and together they are evidenced in the lack of self-control which displays a lack of faith. Being anxious does not make any situation better; rather it worsens an already bad situation. When anxiety matures, it turns into worry and we all know that worry is the seed of failure.

Worry

Worry is perhaps the most unnecessary and unreasonable thing we do. However, we all still do it. It is an unnecessary distraction of the mind. It is neither profitable nor rewarding in any way. It is an exercise in futility and therefore is counter productive in all its manifestations. It has never helped and will never help anyone. Worry is an agonizing feeling. It is like dwelling on something that is in the past and cannot be restored, on something current over which we have no control. Worry is a destructive attitude of the mind that impacts health, peace, and general well-being in negative ways. Why worry when we can pray?

One of the best antidotes to worry that this writer has experienced is the power of prayer. A prayerful preparation prevents anxiety and worry. The late Archbishop Benson Idahosa once said, "Prayerful preparation prevents poor performance." Prayer brings assurance and stabilizes the soul. Prayer causes expectation and positive expectation brings about positive results. Worry always has a negative impact or a negative outcome in every situation. The impact of worry cannot be measured on any scale, but it can be measured against the quality of health, peace, and happiness. Worrying robs us of our well-deserved, God-given joy and peace. We will do well to fight this thief with prayer. It is written in the scripture, "Be anxious for nothing, but in everything by prayer and supplication with thanksgiving let your request be made known to God and the peace of God which surpasses all understanding will guard your heart through Christ Jesus" (Philippians 4:6-7).

Instead of filling our minds with worries, we must fill them with thoughts of good things; with things that encourage, exhort, edify and uplift the soul. "Finally brethren, whatever things are true, whatever things are noble, whatever things are just, whatever things are pure, whatever things are lovely, whatever things are of good report, if there are any virtues, and if there is anything praiseworthy, meditate (think) on these things" (Philippians 4:8). Filling our minds with songs, scriptures, prayer, and other forms of good communication is being proactive. Worrying is reactive and truthfully, no condition will improve with worry. The time and energy spent in worrying can best be spent praying. Living in worry is the opposite of living by grace and faith. The personal question now becomes, "Are you a worrier or are you faith-full?"

How to Stop Worrying

In order to stop worrying, you must engage yourself in positive thoughts and then take action. Here are some suggestions to get you started:

- Write down the subject of concern on a sheet of paper and list all the possible solutions.
- Take action directly against the negative! Disrupt those moments of intensely negative thought by doing things in a different way.
- Remind yourself repeatedly that worry does not and cannot change the situation; in other words, rebuke yourself from that old indulgence

- Making positive plans to resolve the subject of concern by discussing the concern exhaustively on your own or with someone you trust.

And most importantly, pray about the subject of concern by submitting it to the only

One who can provide constant help. Pray without ceasing; pray, *pray*, ***pray*** into existence the desired change; praying as many as ten times, pray for an hour, pray for a day, a week, a month or until the unwanted thought goes away, the prayer is answered, or until something happens to satisfy the need.

Chapter 10

God's Antidote

*H*ave you ever been bitten by a poisonous snake or spider? Were the first words out of your mouth what is the antidote? We are all aware that in the physical realm, if poison enters our body it can do irreparable harm to vital organs and often very quickly. The same is true for the spiritual realm. If we allow the poison of fear, anxiety and worry to course through our bodies, we can do irreparable harm not only to our physical body but also to our ability to complete our destiny assignment. The Apostle Paul could have had his mission to Rome delayed or stopped altogether if he had not known the antidote to the "viper's" bite.

> *But when Paul had gathered a bundle of sticks and laid them on the fire, a viper came out because of the heat and fastened itself on his hand. When the natives saw the creature hanging from his hand, they began saying to one another, "Undoubtedly this man is a murderer, and though he has been saved from the sea, justice has not allowed him to*

live." However he shook the creature off into the fire and suffered no harm. But they were expecting that he was about to swell up or suddenly fall down dead. But after they had waited a long time and had seen nothing unusual happen to him, they changed their minds and began to say that he was a god. (Acts 28:3-6 NAS)

Faith

Has the viper of fear, anxiety or worry bitten you? Faith is the only antidote for fear of which I am aware. Faith is that deep settled assurance inside that knows you have a big Father who is bigger than all the world's problems put together. This God is certainly bigger than your problems. Faith is the opposite or the flip-side of fear. So you either have faith or fear—but not both at the same time. Anytime you are afraid for whatever reason, you can be sure that you do not have faith. Your faith may be small but it is still faith.

Jesus said, "Have faith in God" because He knew that faith must have an anchor (Mark 11:22). Faith does not exist in thin air or in a vacuum. Faith must be anchored on something or someone greater, higher, bigger, and more powerful in all respects than you are. Otherwise, that thing or that person cannot command absolute faith and respect. The same is true of fear. It does not exist in a vacuum. It is always anchored in something over which you have no control.

Faith is absolute trust. It must be absolute to bring down the power and grace of God to bear upon your situation. Partial faith is no faith at all as far as God is concerned. It is better to have a little faith and to be absolute, than to *sort of* have faith. The reason is God does not and will not share His glory or praise with anyone. "I am the Lord, that is my name; and my glory I will not give to another; nor my praise to any graven images" (Isaiah 42:8). You either trust God fully or you do not.

You may argue this assertion, but it is the absolute truth. The scripture says, "But without Faith it is **impossible** to please Him, for he who comes to God must believe that He is, and that He is the Rewarder of those who diligently seek Him" (Hebrews 11:6 emphasis added by author). You cannot seek diligently for something you do not believe is there somewhere. God is the only basis for miracle-producing faith. The reason faith is so crucial in the attainment of grace is because it works by faith, and vice versa. In order to obtain additional grace, favor, miracles or any blessings from God, you must trust Him unconditionally. God is perfect and a perfectionist. Anybody can have faith. In short, everybody has some faith, but it depends on where you want to place it.

I once witnessed a friend who was having problems in many areas of his life, including fear. He was so afraid and concerned that he went to see a voodoo priest. He was not successful in receiving the desired results although he complained that the charges for service were rather high. He became desperate and saw another person sitting on the floor reciting or chanting some words and went to him asking him to pray for a solution to his problems. Of course, he did not receive a solution because he did not know upon whom to call. That was when I introduced him to Jesus because I knew Jesus could help him. He said, "I believe there is a force out there, but this Jesus of a thing, I don't believe it." He left still clinging to his problems. Faith depends on whom or in what you place your trust.

My friend was willing to trust a mere man who had no power to help, but would not put his trust in the Son of God, who could have helped him. Be sure that your faith is anchored on something solid.

Grace in Sickness

Nowhere is the power and benefit of grace more evident than in sickness. There is grace for those who are sick or suffering in sickness and particularly those with terminal illnesses. The focus of grace in sickness is the ability to believe in God for divine healing. By the way, divine healing is still happening today even as you are reading these words. I have personally received abundant grace of divine healing more times than I can count. I have also been a vessel through which divine healings have been offered to other people.

I remember once when I was diagnosed with a sub-acute appendicitis. (I am one of those who fear injections more than a child). My doctor told me to prepare for surgery in about two weeks. I went home that day and could not sleep the whole night. Eventually, I convinced myself that I served a healing God. I decided to take my case to God in prayer and with the antibiotic medicine that I was given, I prayerfully approached my Father. Two weeks came and passed, but I refused to go and see the doctor because I was afraid he would ask me to go in for an operation. I prayed and prayed and believed the Word of God. Within eight weeks my pain subsided completely. God healed me. I have had other health challenges and God has healed me miraculously; sometimes with medication and other times without medication. It basically depended on my faith at a given time and in a particular situation.

The grace of trusting God through sickness is given to everyone who believes in Jesus Christ. However, I am sad to say that many believers have resorted to worrying instead of believing, trusting, and praying. God loves you and wants you to be well. Trusting God helps you to focus on why and how the sickness developed, the wrong things you've done or what you did not do at all. It will help you find out whether the sickness was as a result of some past or present sins. It will help you to check if anger, resentment, bitterness, un-forgiveness or frustrations were contributing factors.

Trusting God will help you search your spirit to confess and renounce any hidden sins that might hinder your prayers and other peoples' prayers for you. Sometimes sickness comes from what we eat or indulge in. These grace-exercises of soul searching can help bring healing or can be managed through your emotions. With this done, you will have free and unfettered access to the throne of grace and your healing will come quickly. Read carefully what God says in Isaiah 58:6-9.

> *Is this not the fast that I have chosen? To loose the bonds of wickedness, to undo the heavy burdens, to let the oppressed go free, and that you break every yoke. Is it not to share your bread with the hungry, and that you bring to your house the poor who are cast out; when you see the naked that you cloth him, and not to hide yourself from your own flesh? Then your light shall break forth like the morning, your healing shall spring forth speedily, and your righteousness shall go before you; the glory of the Lord shall be your rear guard. Then you shall call*

and the Lord will answer; and you shall cry and the Lord shall say, "Here I am."

This process has helped me many times to discover some of the root causes of my problems. It helps you free your mind so that divine healing can come faster. Divine healing only comes after forgiveness has taken place. That makes it a double-barreled blessing because you receive physical, emotional, and spiritual healings. Once in a doctor's office in Nigeria, I saw an inscription written on a plaque that read, "We care, but God heals." Those five words capture the main essence of modern medicine, and it helped me to change and re-focus my faith more on God when I am sick or afflicted. Taking problems to Jesus and casting every burden on God will help to eliminate anxiety and worry.

Dr. Bernie S. Siegel, M.D., said in his foreword for the book *Prayer, Faith and Healing* by Kenneth Winston Caine and Brian Paul Kaufman, "The will to live is physiological, and when you connect with your spiritual essence, it is felt in every aspect of your life and every cell in your body." By the way, that book, *Prayer, Faith and Healing*, is by far the best book I ever read on healing and prayer. It documents with scientific evidences, the power and effects of prayer and faith in the lives of thousands of sick people. It is written with such clarity and completeness that you will not only find faith for your need, but also very important information for other purposes in life. I very highly recommend it.

When we pray with faith God hears, and when He hears He answers and gives grace. God hears every prayer. He sees a broken and contrite heart. He does not despise but promises to those who come to Him that He will never cast anyone out or reject them (see Psalm 51:17 and John 6:37). God's glory cannot be revealed until the prayers are made. One of the main purposes of Jesus' coming to the earth is revealed in Luke 4:18-19, "The Spirit of the Lord is upon Me, because He has anointed Me to preach the gospel to the poor, He has sent Me to heal the broken hearted, to preach deliverance to the captives and recovering of sight to the blind, to set at liberty those who are oppressed."

Sometimes when we are sick, we doubt whether God can heal us. John the Baptist also doubted whether Jesus was the expected Messiah, the Deliverer, and he sent his own disciples to find out who Jesus really was. Jesus responded simply, "Go and tell John the things you have seen and heard; that the blind see, the lame walk, the lepers are cleansed, the dead are raised, the poor have the gospel preached to them" (Luke 7:22).

Jesus is still doing the same things today through His Spirit. There is no sickness or disease so great that God cannot cure. The only limiting factor is the lack of faith and persistence in prayer. Some people are willing to stay on medication that can only minimize their pain for the rest of their lives, rather than knock continuously on the door of Him who has the power, ability, and the spare parts to heal and repair an ailing body. Prayer is as powerful as any medication and more beneficial because it leaves no side effects. Medication *combined* with prayer works wonders!

Every illness has a measure of grace. The greater the depth of your sickness, the greater is the release of grace to bear and pull you through to a healthy life. I have seen children go through hardships to which adults without grace would easily succumb. While God does not necessarily give sickness, He sometimes allows disease to test and/or discipline us. In such cases, He says "My grace is sufficient for you, for My strength is made perfect in weakness."

If you are reading this book and are stricken with sickness, I believe God has a plan to heal you. With anchored faith, God can heal you miraculously, however, if faith waivers He can still heal you through a combination of faith, medications and prayer.

Divine Healing

Is any among you afflicted? Let him pray. Is any merry? Let him sing psalms. Is any sick among you? Let him call the elders of the church; and let them pray over him, anointing him with oil in the name of the Lord: And the prayer of faith shall save the sick, and the Lord shall raise him up; and if he has committed any sin, they shall be forgiven him. Confess your faults one to another, and pray for one another, that you may be healed. The effective fervent prayer of the righteous man avails much. Elijah was a man with a nature like ours, and he prayed earnestly that it should not rain, and it did not rain on the land for three years and six months. And he prayed again, and the heaven gave rain and the earth produced its fruit. (James 5:13-18)

Ever since I came to understand divine healing or that God still heals today, I have chosen that option above any other form of healing. Of course, I do avail myself of every clean and orthodox means of healing, but I rely very heavily on divine healing because I have personally proved beyond every doubt that it is the *best* form of healing. It does not leave any side effects, is least expensive, and the incidence of the sickness coming back again is negligible. I also choose it because it is what I can do myself without exposing myself to the opinions of other people.

What I know is if you believe in Jesus the Healer, and continuously, persistently pray for healing, you will receive it because God is no respecter of persons. Moreover, I have been using this method for over thirty years and I can tell you with certainty that it works. However, not all sicknesses are healed in the same way. If God is allowing it for a test or discipline, it may not go away when you wish, but you will have the grace to go through it. Even as I was in the process of writing this book, I received healing of a pain in my right leg and the right side of my body. I was diagnosed with what the doctors called a *foot spur*. This affliction was giving me incredible pain all through the right side of my body and under my right foot. I sometimes limped when I walked. It was very painful, especially when I first woke up in the morning and when I was driving my car. I went in for an X-ray which showed that there was a growth inside and under my foot. I was referred to a Chiropodist (foot doctor) who recommended a special type of shoe.

I asked if there was a cure for the growth, and he said, "No, but if the problem gets worse, you may have to be operated on and even then, there is no guarantee of a complete cure."

As I indicated before, I am one of those who fear the needle very much and I cannot stand the sight of blood. Hearing that there was no remedy or available cure for my problem was the last thing I wanted to hear. I went to God in prayer because I knew that God is a specialist in impossibilities. Jesus said, "The things which are impossible with men are possible with God" (Luke 18:27). That was less than two months ago in April of this year. As I am writing these words, I confess to the glory of the healing God that I am healed. The pain is gone and I now walk well without any pain. This goes to show the process of God's healing still continues.

This is just one of the many, many healing miracles I have received on a regular basis. I testify that divine healing is real and available to all who believe. Please, I do not want you to be deceived into thinking that all prayers are answered the same way. But one thing I know from my own experience and from those that I have prayed for is that God heals. God answers prayer!

In James 5:13-18 tell us how to be healed when we are sick. It is as simple as that. There is nothing complicated about it at all. God made healing so easy and simple that anybody can access it. If your problem is one you think you can handle alone, or with God's help, then pray for it. But if it is bigger than your faith can handle then go to your pastor who will determine whether you both together can handle it or whether it would be necessary to call the elders of the church to come and pray together with you. However, if your church or organization does not believe in divine healing, look for another pastor that does believe in this miracle. This writer would be glad and willing to pray with you "the effective, fervent prayer" for your healing. I always use these scriptures as affirmations and "thought blockers" to thwart bad and unwanted thoughts.

Chapter 11

Grace in Sin: Grace for Sinners

But if we walk in the light as He is in the light, we have fellowship with one another, and the blood of Jesus Christ His Son cleanses us from all sin. If we say that we have no sin, we deceive ourselves, and the truth is not in us. If we confess our sins, He is faithful and just to forgive us our sins and to cleanse us from all unrighteousness. If we say that we have not sinned, we make Him a liar, and His word is not in us. (1 John 1:7-10)

Romans 5:20 - *Moreover the Law entered that the offence might abound. But where sin abounded, grace abounded much more.*

Romans 5:8 - *But God demonstrated His love toward us, in that while we were yet sinners (in sin), Christ died for us.*

Titus 2:11 - *For the grace of God that brings salvation has appeared unto all men, teaching us that denying ungodliness and worldly lust, we should live soberly and righteously and godly in this present age, looking for the blessed hope and the glorious appearing of our great God and Savior Jesus Christ.*

Ephesians 2:8 - *For by grace are you saved through faith, and that is not of yourselves; it is the gift of God, not of works, lest any man should boast.*

Titus 3:5 - *Not by works of righteousness which we have done but according to His mercy He saved us.*

These and many more scriptures tell us of God's love for sinners and how much grace is available for sinners and those living in sin. The main reason Jesus came to earth was to save, redeem, restore, purchase, forgive, help emancipate sinners and those trapped in the vicious cycle of sin and Satan. That was His mandate from the Father. "For this purpose the Son of God was manifested that He might destroy the works of the devil" (1 John 3:8). Ever since then the Master has been faithfully fulfilling that mandate. No other ministry of Jesus or His followers has been more important or has received more prominence. Even now in Heaven, Jesus is still praying and interceding on behalf of sinners.

God does not want any of His children to perish. "The Lord is not slack concerning His promise, as some count slackness, but is long suffering toward us, not willing that any should perish but that all should come to repentance" (2 Peter 3:9). The heartbeat of God is for sinners to repent and return to Him. To achieve this purpose God came down in human form to meet with man one-on-one, to talk, reason and understand our point of view, and bring man back to Himself because He loves man so very much. On top of that, He declared a general amnesty to all. He forgave everyone's past, present and future sins just for the asking, and set us free by His actions on the cross. He left His Holy Spirit, the spirit of Jesus Christ, behind in the world to help, convince, motivate, encourage, convict, persuade, remind, and receive the sinner's prayer no matter how simple it might be.

Not satisfied with that, He sent and continues to send men and women today to people that have never known, seen or heard of Jesus or Christianity. They go with little or no support from anyone across deserts, seas, oceans, to the tops of mountain, and into unknown caves. They also go by radio, television and the internet. Many who cannot go physically send people, money, resources, and gifts. Still others spend countless hours of intercession and prayer to save a soul like yours and mine.

In Heaven God is still delaying the hour of His return to see one more soul saved. Will you be the next soul to come to Jesus? God is doing everything possible to reach you and your loved ones. Please, will you do God and someone else a favor and give a copy of this book to that loved one with a request to "Read it to the end." God is not mad or angry with anyone regardless of where you have been, what you have done or what you are doing now. He only wants you back. It will break His heart through all eternity to see you perish and be lost forever without His grace. He wants you back so much that He has even sent me, of all people, to talk to you through this medium. Please, do not say *no* to Him. He loves you very much. I know you have heard this message many times, but this time it is different. It is my urgent message to you. Do not let this be your last chance.

God loves you and He would not want to see any of His children make the same costly and eternal mistakes that others have foolishly made. "Be wise, therefore, and respond to God's love and grace and you will have peace and eternal life with Jesus our Great Master and Lord. God's grace for sinners is undoubtedly His best and costliest because it is Christ, in you, the hope of glory" (Colossians 1:27 MSG).

Sin Is a Heavy Load

For my iniquities have gone over my head; like a heavy burden they are too heavy for me. (Psalm 38:4)

Sin that is not confessed is a very heavy load to carry. Anyone who has committed a serious sin in the past and carried a burden of guilt knows that sin is a heavy load. When that load is taken away, we feel very light in our spirit and the joy and peace of salvation returns. Hear what David, the psalmist said, "Restore unto me the joy of your salvation" (Psalm 51:12). David lost his joy when he committed a very serious sin. Most people have lost joy and peace and do not know how to get back on course.

When we commit a very serious sin and fail to confess it, we lose our joy, peace and our spirit is saddened and sick. Even the mind will be affected and our health will deteriorate physically, mentally, emotionally, and spiritually. If it continues this way and more sins are added, consequences can be unpredictable and are often unrelated to the original sin. This can lead to other problems such as sleeplessness, drinking, prostitution, drugs, multiple killings, and other acts of irresponsibility. That is why the message of grace should be preached much more in the denominational churches.

When people feel that there is no way out of their guilt problem, sometimes they become hardened in their ways and go all out to do evil. For others, they may break down under the weight of their sin and guilt and become sick. When guilt is mixed with fear, worry and anxiety, it can tear down the health and immune systems of the body and can result in sicknesses. These illnesses are very hard to detect even with powerful microscopes and modern medical tests. Serious spiritual sins such as forgiveness and bitterness, when mixed with the guilt of one or more serious crimes or sins, can be a platform for spiritual and emotional attacks.

The weight of sin is so heavy that it weighs down the spirit, the soul and the body's defenses. It makes you feel angry and become frustrated. These feelings can easily be passed on to other people because a frustrated person is an angry person. No one can understand this better than the person whose sins have been forgiven and the guilt has been lifted. Different types of sin affect people differently. Some sins are easily overcome, but the individuals are so overwhelmed by this guilt, they can carry it with them to the grave. Regardless of their unbendable nature, they remain under a perpetual torment because sin creates torment, while grace gives peace and joy. A good prayer to say when you are feeling guilt and torment is found in Psalm 51. I will present it here for easy access.

Grace in Sin: Grace for Sinners

Psalm 51

*To the chief Musician: A Psalm of
David when Nathan, the prophet,
went to him, after he had gone in to Bath-sheba.
Have mercy upon me, O God,
According to Your loving kindness;
According to the multitude of Your tender mercies,
Blot out my transgressions.
Wash me thoroughly from my iniquity,
And cleanse me from my sin.*

*For I acknowledge my transgressions,
And my sin is always before me.
Against You, You only, have I sinned,
And done this evil in Your sight—
That You may be found just when You speak,
And blameless when You judge.*

*Behold, I was brought forth in iniquity,
And in sin my mother conceived me.
Behold, You desire truth in the inward parts,
And in the hidden part You will make me
to know wisdom.*

*Purge me with hyssop, and I shall be clean;
Wash me, and I shall be whiter than snow.
Make me hear joy and gladness,
That the bones You have broken may rejoice.
Hide Your face from my sins,
And blot out all my iniquities.*

Create in me a clean heart, O God,
And renew a steadfast spirit within me.
Do not cast me away from Your presence,
And do not take Your Holy Spirit from me.

Restore to me the joy of Your salvation,
And uphold me by Your generous Spirit.
Then I will teach transgressors Your ways,
And sinners shall be converted to You.

Deliver me from the guilt of bloodshed, O God,
The God of my salvation,
And my tongue shall sing aloud of Your righteousness.
O Lord, open my lips,
And my mouth shall show forth Your praise.
For You do not desire sacrifice, or else I would give it;
You do not delight in burnt offering.
The sacrifices of God are a broken spirit,
A broken and a contrite heart—
These, O God, You will not despise.

Do good in Your good pleasure to Zion;
Build the walls of Jerusalem.
Then You shall be pleased with the sacrifices of righteousness,
With burnt offering and whole burnt offering;
Then they shall offer bulls on Your altar. (NKJV)

This Psalm has helped me personally and has helped many clients that I have counseled. I am blessed by God with a gift of spiritual insight with discernment into spiritual problems. Do not allow your sin to weigh or break you down. You can prayerfully take advantage of the above Psalm and break free into the light and liberty of the grace, peace, and joy of the Lord. Sin is a very heavy load to bear, so do not continue to carry it. Jesus paid for your deliverance and He stands by ready to carry it away from you if you will only ask. "He that covers his sin will not prosper but whoever confesses and forsakes them will have (receive) mercy" (Proverbs 28:13 NKJV).

Why Grace Is Not Preached More in Churches

I believe that the reason grace is not preached as often as it should be in the churches is because preachers believe it will lead people to commit more sin, to backslide, or to take the grace of God for granted. Others believe that you must work out your salvation with fear and trembling; in other words, you must keep the laws to receive and/or maintain your salvation. Yet others believe the message of grace is too simplistic because we cannot go to Heaven by accepting Jesus with just a two-minute sinner's prayer and other such reasoning.

I must say that all those reasons are cogent, reasonable and good, but if God marks our sins, who (including pastors, bishops and the Pope) will stand? Jesus said, "Come unto me all you that labor and are heavy laden and I will give you rest" (Matthew 11:28). Paul said in 1 Timothy 1:15, "This is a faithful saying and worthy of all acceptance, that Christ Jesus came into the world to save sinners of whom I am the chief." When Jesus walked on this earth He forgave sins and sinners left, right, and centre. He said to the man who had paralysis (palsy), "Son, your sin is forgiven you…but that you may know that the Son of Man has power on earth to forgive sins"—He said to the paralytic, "I say to you, arise, take up your bed, and go to your house" (Mark 2:5,10-11 NKJV). Jesus also said in Mark 2:17, "Those who are well have no need of physician, but those that are sick. I did not come to call the righteous but sinners to repentance." (Mark 2:17 NKJV).

The fact that people are not so much aware of the grace of God makes them sin more and when they sin they begin to run from God. More often than not these people find it difficult to come back because they think that God will not forgive them or because they have gone too far. God's grace has provided an advocate or attorney with the Father, this same Jesus, to plead our case in the presence God. Hear the Father's heartbeat from the Apostle John, "My little Children, these things I write to you that you may not sin. And if anyone sins, we have an advocate with the Father, Jesus Christ the righteous. And He Himself is our propitiation for our sins, and not for ours only but also for the whole world" (1 John 2:1-2). If a person's sins are so great that he must be taken to the High Court of God, there is already an advocate, an attorney per excellence, who died in the sinner's place. Jesus, as his attorney, will stand in his place, plead his case, squash his conviction, set him free, and then give him eternal life.

Dear friend, I did not write these things. They are there for you to see for yourself so that you can understand and learn how much God loves the sinner, even though He hates sin with a passion. No matter where you are right now, whether backsliding or if you don't know or understand the Christian faith, God is there for you. God loves you anyway. God wants His children to know Him. He wants to forgive you and give you peace. In His infinite wisdom, He has done all there is to do to make peace between the two of you. He has declared, "There is, therefore, now no condemnation to those who are in Christ Jesus, who walk not after the flesh but after the spirit. For the law of the Spirit of Life in Christ Jesus has made me free from the law of sin and death" (Roman 8:1-2).

God says you are free. Why do you not lift up your hands and say, "Thank you Lord for the love and grace You have extended to me. I give my heart to You, to cleanse and purify me and to make me Your own child in Jesus' name. Amen."

The church is a hospital for sinners, a military hospital, if you will. Those who work there are called saints, but they were all former sinners who were touched by the grace of God. They have been taught and educated in the Gospel, to help care for other wounded and returning sinners. Others were trained to become ambassadors for Christ, the Savior. "Now, therefore, we are ambassadors for Christ, as though God did beseech you by us: we pray for you in Christ's stead, be reconciled to God" (2 Corinthian 5:20). Therefore, there is no reason why the message of grace should not be preached as often as possible so that people may hear and return to the Lord. The period of grace is running out and Jesus will soon be coming back. I personally would not like to go to any church that does not proclaim the message of grace as its major theme.

Grace through Trials, Afflictions or Suffering

There is grace for every human situation, even though many times it does not seem like it. Are you passing through trials, afflictions or suffering? Jesus says, "Come unto me all you who labor and are heavy-laden, and I will give you rest" (Matthew 11:28). In this scripture the word rest also includes peace and contentment. This scripture clearly shows that God understands what you are going through right now. Another scripture says, "For we do not have a high priest who cannot sympathize with our weakness *(feelings)*, but was in all points, tempted as we are, but without sin" (Hebrew 4:15). God understands your situation right now and is very sympathetic. It may not seem so to you because you cannot see His face, but believe His Word because He cares.

Often what we pass through comes as a result of temptation from the devil or as a trial from the Lord to teach us something to make us stronger. Sometimes our discomfort comes as a result of our mistakes. Regardless of the source, God says, "I will be with him (you) in trouble… He shall call upon me and I will answer him: I will deliver him and honor him" (Psalm 91:15 author paraphrase). In fact all of Psalm 91 is about God's comfort for those who are under distress. I recommend that you not only read it but memorize it if you can. He is always there in any and every situation that you face, especially if you have made Jesus your Lord and Savior. I always find hope and comfort in this Psalm.

Chapter 12

Vision Driven Grace Life

"*W*here there is no revelation, the people cast off restraint" (Proverbs 29:18 NKJV). The word revelation here is also often translated as vision. A man without a vision is like a plane without a compass. A revelation or a vision is a word that many people do not really understand in many Christian circles. Is there any such thing as God-given vision? How do I know what my vision is? So really, what is a vision?

Vision according to the Oxford Advanced Learner's Dictionary is:

- The ability to see
- The area you can see from a particular position
- An idea or picture in your imagination
- A dream or similar experience, especially, of a religious type
- The ability to think about or plan the future with great imagination and intelligence, etc.

Vision, in our case, speaks about the special combination of skills, imagination and intelligence, to see things in your spirit, articulate them in the natural world, and make adequate and comprehensive plans that bring them forth into reality. It is a special God-given ability or grace to dream an idea with your imagination, transmute the intangible impulses of your thoughts into a living hope, and then create an organized plan that carries with it a consuming passion to bring it to realization. It is tapping into the Divine resources within you and harnessing the infinite, intangible, and often spiritual forces to come up with an idea and passion for something unique and original to you.

Everybody in this world has the potential to unlock the creative genius within them and take the resources of their Divine intelligence and create an idea that is unique, original and new. This special creative ability comes with a special desire and burning passion that will never go away until it finds expression and fulfillment. If the idea is from the Spirit, it will keep you uncomfortably motivated and passionate until it is accomplished or achieved. The desire to be unique or special is innate in all of us. This uniqueness is also brought to bear in the way we think. Vision-driven grace is a gift from God. It is the gift that sets you or will set you apart from all other people on the planet once it is discovered, harnessed, and delivered. It will give you the fulfillment of a lifetime, and a sense of accomplishment that will enrich and make you popular. This grace is deposited within you from birth. It is written in your DNA and in your destiny. Some people discover their true vision from childhood and others later in life.

The grace-driven vision releases favor, and opens the door of unlimited opportunities for you. Once discovered and pursued, people will see the grace in you and all the resources and people that have been assigned to help you accomplish that vision/project will begin to fall into place at the right time and in the right place. Furthermore, no one can stop it. At the appropriate time, even old enemies may become friends and strangers will become allies. That does not mean that there will be no difficulties or problems. The enemy likes to send distractions that can permanently derail the entire process or betrayals by those who were not meant to be in the loop in the first place. But if the vision has gathered enough momentum and passion, it will remain on course regardless of the difficulties encountered.

Vision is the seed of an idea and an idea is the foundation of every achievement. You sow a vision and you reap an idea. Without a new idea nothing *new* would happen. Every good idea that is properly sowed in good soil will produce infinite results. And let me say that 'Money follows every good idea' and it's not the other way round. This is the age of ideas and the next age will see unbelievable new ideas and inventions.

What Is an Idea?

An idea is a thought, concept or conceptualization, "guess-timation," hunch, suggestion or vision of something you plan to do. It is an impression or picture in your imagination that needs to be clothed in word and action. New ideas are only as good as the faith that's behind them. Without faith, no idea can survive. A strong faith gives birth to a strong and power-full idea. A powerful idea comes with momentum, passion, and purpose. These are the driving forces behind every successful idea. The power of an idea can only be imagined, you can be sitting on a million dollar idea without knowing it. You cannot know what an idea is worth until it is born, clothed in words, actions, and then tested.

Most people kill their good ideas before they have the chance to see the light of day. Fear may cause others to leave their newly birthed ideas in the incubator until they die. Still others give birth to good, but weak and feeble ideas with no faith-base behind them, so they never make it in the world of competitive ideas. There is no vision without an idea. One good idea can change your life and move you from a pauper to a millionaire. Every unborn idea is worth at least a million dollars, so you can see how much you may be losing or have lost. This writer had a simple idea that turned into a million dollar business.

A Million Dollar Idea

In 1988 I lost my job as a sales executive with a subsidiary of a French conglomerate, in Lagos, Nigeria, called Technology and Systems (SCOA). I thought to myself, if I could put the same amount of time and energy into doing something for myself, I could earn a living and better myself. Because I did not have any savings, I decided to put on my good and positive thinking cap and let my imagination run wild. I wrote down every thought that came into my mind, even including stealing, to raise the capital to start a business.

As I was doing all this thinking, I remembered the question God asked Moses from the burning bush, "What do you have in your hand?" Moses said, "A rod." God said, "Cast it to the ground." When Moses did the rod became a serpent. God told him to take the serpent by the tail, and when he did it became a rod again in his hand (author paraphrase of Exodus 4:1-4).

Meanwhile, I was looking at a specially woven native "Akwete Cloth" that I bought for my wife. As I thought more on Moses' encounter with God, I began to see a connection with that cloth. There were actually several of those cloths. So I began to think if I could sell those materials, I could make some profit and earn enough capital to buy back the cloth for my wife before she returned home from her vacation. As I became convinced that this was the best and easiest way to raise enough capital to start a little business, I decided to act quickly. I was a salesman so I knew the city well, but the business of selling women's clothing was something I never thought of before and certainly was not my specialty. However, my idea had so much momentum, passion, and drive that I could not resist it.

The next day I packed four of those cloths in my briefcase, dressed corporately in my suit and tie, and took off at exactly the same time I normally left for the office to meet my first client at 9:00 AM. I went to two offices and met two fashion designers as my grace for the day shone very brightly. When I went into the third fashion designer, it was like a divine appointment. The name of the place was Mofechi. As if she was expecting me, the director left what she was doing and came to meet me personally. We briefly exchanged pleasantries and she asked me who I was looking for. I never met her before so I said, "The manager."

She asked, "What for?"

I said, "I have some fashion materials that she might love to see."

Then, with eagerness in her eyes, she said, "Let's see it."

As I opened my briefcase and brought out all I had, she became very excited and bought all four samples of my material and asked for more. I told her I had two more samples at home and she bought those two, and paid cash for them all. We then entered into a non-binding agreement for a steady supply of those materials. In less than three hours, I made a profit that was more than one month's salary at my previous job *and* I was home again by noon. This was the initial idea of a business that became a million-dollar company.

In three years, this little "kitchen business" grew and was recognized by the local and the State Chambers of Commerce, The Federal Ministry of Industry, and The Commonwealth. The State Government of Abia approved an acre of land for the proposed expansion of this new business. At the height of the business, it employed thirty-seven workers at the factory site, and six management officers in Aba and Lagos. Later, the factory was sold for more than two million in Nigerian Niara (Nigerian currency).

The Word of God is my inspiration in everything I do, even though I still have my own share of poor ideas sometimes.

Bad Ideas

There are as many bad ideas as there are good ones. However, bad ideas appear to have an edge over good ideas. Some people find it easier to act on their bad ideas rather than on their good ones. People prefer to lie rather than to tell the truth, cheat rather than to be honest, hate rather than to love, fight and divorce rather than to settle, and waste time rather than to put time to a useful purpose. Some even choose to destroy rather than to build, steal and kill rather than to protect. The list of bad ideas is endless. The good news is that it takes about the same amount of energy to conceive a bad idea as it takes to create a good one.

So why are people so prone to bad ideas rather than to good ones? The answer is simple. It is the mindset. Proverbs 23:7 says, "As a man thinks in his heart so is he..." (Proverbs 23:7 NKJV). If you tune your mind to think evil, most likely your actions will be evil. If you set your mind to think good and positive ideas, the result of the actions that follow will bring about good.

The good news is that at least one out of the millions of positive, progressive, and well-thought-out ideas you have could one day make you a millionaire or at least pull you out of your present situation. It will only happen if you decide to act upon it. Good ideas mixed with strong, faithful action will change your life for the better. Remember that money follows every good idea if it is properly presented and acted upon.

New Ideas

New ideas are the products of new and highly energized, well organized, time-tested and thought-trend processes. An enriched idea can result in new breakthroughs, inventions and profitable business ventures that offer many underlying opportunities. But they do not come haphazardly. It must first be received in the spirit, painstakingly thought through, incubated in the mind for quite some time, and be purpose-driven. It must be acceptable, beneficial to a target audience, and make a lot of sense to would-be stockholders. If you want something new to be happening to you all the time, you must envision new ideas and then the financing will follow.

I have always said and strongly believe that money and resources will follow every good idea. There is no shortage of money, but good ideas are in short supply. A good idea, properly packaged and presented, will attract an equivalent amount of money to support it. Money will always follow a good idea.

The benefits of new ideas are many. They will:

- Keep your heart bubbling with joy
- Keep your mind positively engaged
- Provide you with tools to better your life
- Sharpen your imaginative faculties
- Strengthen your intellectual abilities
- Give you a sense of fulfillment
- Keep your mind young and fresh
- Bring you hope, and so much more!

A new idea is something you have never thought of before, something fresh from your thought vibrations. It comes with a new and elevated energy level that crystallizes in your thought processes and has the living seed of the breath of life. The same breathe of life that God used to create the world. A new idea will move, inspire and motivate you and others to action. It has power, grace, hope, beauty, enthusiasm, and the potential to affect and bless a multitude of people. The more the idea has the ability to bless people, the easier, better and quicker it can attract money. It does not matter if the idea is a toothpick or bottled water, tangible or intangible, the end result is the same. There is always a reward for every good idea.

Chapter 13

Grace for the Dying

Just as there is grace for the living, there is also grace for the dying. Death and dying are two situations in life that no one wants to talk or think about, including yours truly. In fact, it was nowhere in my imagination before I started to write this book. I am one person that loves life and wants to live it to the fullest extent that God allows. Therefore, writing this section of the chapter is not my cup of tea. I do not even consider myself competent in any way to talk about death because I have not really witnessed many deaths first hand, although I have seen a few terminal or dying moments. I have buried the dead, including my own parents.

However, through the grace given to me, I will try to present to you what I know and the inspiration I have received concerning this subject. According to Shakespeare, "Death is a necessary **end**, it will come when it will come." Because death and dying are not kitchen-table discussions and there has always been strong apprehension and fear surrounding death it is hardly ever discussed at home or in schools. Our churches also talk about death mostly in terms of the euphoria of Heaven. But, in reality, death and dying are very serious subjects that evoke strong emotions of fear, loss, and eternal separation.

For these and other reasons, it is important to help people understand that there is grace also in dying. There is as much grace in dying as in living. The same God that made the birth of a new baby glorious is the same God that will make our spiritual bodies even more glorious at death and thereafter. The pain of dying is mostly as a result of the fear and sense of loss or eternal separation from what we have loved, worked for, possessed, and lived for. The second reason is the fear of not knowing exactly what it will be like; whether there is Heaven and hell, and, if they exist, whether we are going to Heaven or hell.

The purpose of this chapter is to help those who are terminally ill and others who might not know how to face the subject of death. I want my readers to receive some insight into this special topic. God does not want His beloved children to have a harrowing experience at the best time of our lives and that is what death is - *the best time of life*. It is the graduation period of all our studies, toils, and pleasures in this world. Like the end of an academic pursuit in high school or college, some students feel very happy and cannot wait for the last paper, while others are apprehensive and are not sure what is next. Some look toward graduation with great anticipation while others are not so sure and even dread it.

No matter to which camp you belong to, you must exit one day. "And as it is appointed unto men once to die and after that judgment" (Hebrews 9:27). It has already been pre-determined by the Higher Power. You cannot avoid it, escape it, refuse it or buy your way around it. It is a constant; it is a universal law. It is irrevocable, inescapable, and unchangeable. So why struggle with it? Every wise person should expect death at any time, and factor that intentionally into the scheme of things. Children, youth, young adults, the mature and the grey haired all die. Knowing and accepting that as fact gives everyone the opportunity to confess their sins, and make peace and amends for the things you know and feel you have not done well.

The good thing for those who know in advance of their impending departure from this earth is they have time to prepare themselves, set their house in order, confess their sins, and make peace with their Creator. Once these things are completed, they can depart joyfully even though sometimes it is with pain. The pain of death is the last discomfort of this life. It is a mixture of joy and pain. Joy because you are going to your real home to rest and to see Jesus, the One who loved you so much that He risked everything to die and save you. There is pain because the process of dying is like the process of pregnancy and birth. When a baby is about to be born, there are all kinds of discomforts to both the mother and the unborn child. Both of them go through adjustments, pain, and discomfort in preparation for the day of delivery. The day of delivery is a day of joy, but the process of childbirth is not. So it is with the process of death and dying. Death will come one day. Make no mistake about it. Do no wait to put your affairs in order until the last day. Always be prepared as each passing day brings us closer to the D-day.

Too much uncontrollable grieving seems to suggest that the griever, whether the one dying or the one left behind, has no hope of a better life, resurrection or life with Christ. It suggests that the griever has more hope in the dying person than in the Living God.

Behold I tell you a mystery: We shall not all sleep, but we shall be changed; in a moment, in the twinkling of an eye, at the last trumpet. For the trumpet shall sound and the dead shall be raised, and we shall be changed. For this corruptible must put on incorruption, and this mortal must put on immortality. So when this corruptible has put on incorruption and this mortality has put on immortality, then shall be brought to pass the saying that is written: "Death is swallowed up in victory. O death where is your sting? O grave where is your victory." (1 Corinthians 15:50-56)

But I do not want you to be ignorant, brethren, concerning those who have fallen asleep, lest you sorrow as those who have no hope. For if we believe that Jesus died and rose again, even so, God will bring with Him those who sleep in Jesus. For this we say to you by the word of the Lord, that we, who are alive and remain until the coming of the Lord, will by no means precede those who are asleep. For the Lord Himself shall descend from heaven with a shout and with the voice of the archangel, and with the trumpet of God. And the dead in Christ shall rise first. Then we who are alive and remain shall be caught up together with them in the clouds to meet the Lord in the air. And thus we shall always be with the Lord. Therefore, comfort one another with these words." (1 Thessalonians 4:13-18)

The Bible calls death by its rightful name which is *sleep*, a long sleep. We all know that sleep is healthy and medicinal. And if we do not sleep for a couple of days we may become sick or sicker. Allowing or sustaining someone whose time has come, to keep on living is counter productive. Not only is it a drain on our resources, it is also denying the person a well-deserved rest. Eventually the person will become useless while on a life support machine. In no way does that mean, however, that those whose time has not come, (those who can be saved or restored to life) should not use the technology of life support machines. What we are saying here is that those who need the rest of dying more than the pleasure of living should be allowed to sleep on.

Dying is a preparatory process and should be embraced with joy and hope. This will ameliorate the suffering, pain and uncertainties of the last days and moments of life. This will lead to a peaceful and even joyous transition to the world beyond. It will also mitigate the pain, sufferings, and uncertainties of the loved ones who will be left behind. The worst mistake that the dying, homebound, and transitioning people make is to struggle against the process. I believe that every person who is terminally ill, and knows and sees the approach of the day, should tell their loved ones they are ready to expire, but because of fear they usually do not. The closer the approach of death, the more they feel an intense emotion and desire to remain instead of letting go and relieving themselves and their loved ones by shortening this time of emotional distress.

Death should be a peaceful exit. It should be devoid of fear, stress, anxiety or worry. It is a natural process that should not be resisted if it comes naturally and at an old age. Those around the dying should give the individual peace, and time to concentrate, because it is sometimes not easy for the one who is not prepared for death to accept the approach of this reality. The best atmosphere to create around a dying person is to sing or play soft music, pray, and provide encouragement in whatever form the dying person enjoyed while in good health. Experience has shown me that dying people love prayer; the prayer of repentance and forgiveness. On the other hand, Godly people who have accepted and made peace with Christ love songs and hymns, especially their favorite songs that include words of consolation and transition from the world to the next.

The best gift you can ever give to a dying person is to lead him to Christ even if it's at the last minute. If you don't feel qualified, find a pastor or priest to help. No gift can be greater. Most dying people who did not make peace with the Lord previously are ready to do this toward the end of their life when the opportunity is properly presented. There are also those who thought their sins were so great that God could not forgive them. Those people struggle through life until it is their time to die. Others bear bitterness and do not know how to forgive. They cannot let go of life and they may struggle through the narrow passage of the death canal. For those who become sick for a short while before death, it is a great opportunity for them to settle issues with God and with their relatives, friends and acquaintances.

I believe God purposely slotted that period at life's end so people can recognize the approaching exit and can make peace with their Creator and prepare to meet Him again face-to-face. The scripture says, "Prepare to meet your God" (Amos 4:12). The opportunity is sometimes lost because of fear and the struggle to remain longer on earth when God is warning and pleading with the dying person to prepare to come Home. Death is a good thing especially if the dying person understands how important sickness is in the process of dying. It is written, "Precious in the sight of the Lord is the death of His saints" (Psalms 116:15). Loved ones who sense that death is approaching should be strong and encourage the exiting loved one to make peace with God, and be cheerful rather than become angry and show obvious signs of despair.

Another great mistake that people make is to think that the death of a loved one would mean the end of *good* life for the living. There is grace for the living left behind by the exit of a loved one. "God will supply all your needs according to His riches in glory by Christ Jesus" (Philippians 4:19). We are not to make anybody our *source* in this life. Everyone that comes into this world is fully equipped to live and survive even without a mother or father. Loved ones are given to provide comfort and support and to assist us in our journey through this world. They should never take the place of God who is our real source and Provider. We must turn to God and say, "Lord, where and which is the way forward." I believe God knows the time of exit of every person in this world and makes adequate provision for the living.

Grace for dying is evident when you watch two categories of people. You will see a vast difference between a true believer and an unbeliever as they go through the last days, hours, and minutes of their lives. In the true believer, they may quietly rejoice and in some cases they even see angels who have come to escort them home. They present no additional heart breaking scenes and utterances to the living. For those that don't know Jesus and have wickedness in their heart, there is usually a dreaded agony as the end approaches.

When I was a young boy, I knew a powerful chief in my hometown that did not die for many weeks. The family members had to bring in powerful medicine men (witch doctors) to make sacrifices and incantations to release him before he would finally give up his ghost. I knew of another person who would not die, even though the flesh had begun to rot from her body while she was still breathing. I also heard of one person who consistently yelled, "Fire! Fire!" until she took her last breath. The Bible says, "Precious in the sight of the Lord is the death of his saints" (Psalm 116:15). God gives graces to the dying who believe in Christ with all their hearts, have confessed their sins and received forgiveness. The contrary is the case with evil-doers and unrepentant sinners. God is not willing and does not want anyone to perish, but that all should repent.

Chapter 14

The Joy of Living by Grace

*G*race is a mystery. It is an anomaly because it runs contrary to human common sense. Everybody hopefully reaps what they sowed. Everyone should suffer the consequences of their actions and sins. Everyone should get what they deserve. In the Nigerian Pigeon English, a saying goes thus: "Do Me - I Do You - God No Go Vex" in other words it is "tit for tat." The Old Testament encouraged a way of life that we often would like to use to describe this concept. "But if any lasting harm follows, then you shall give life for life, eye for eye, tooth for tooth, hand for hand, foot for foot, burn for burn, wound for wound, stripe for stripe" (Exodus 21:24). In plain English, we only want to love our friends, hate our enemies, do good to those who do good to us.

Unfortunately, this is the way humans think. We like to see the offender duly punished, the sinner go to hell, and the merciless treated mercilessly. These are natural ways of thinking and natural responses to evil and unkindness. But the difference about grace is that the reverse is the case. Grace says *forgive* the sinner, *turn* the other cheek, *do no harm* to your neighbor and *go* the extra mile. What if he asks for your coat? Give a shirt also and if your enemy hungers, give him food to eat. Do not repay evil with evil. Consider yourself, and "let him who thinks he is standing take heed lest he falls" (1 Corinthians 10:12).

Grace gives mercy and kindness to the offender and the sinner. Those who deserve to die are pardoned. The just one dies for the unjust one. Christ died to save sinners.

> *Jesus said, "You have heard that it was said, 'You shall love your neighbor and hate your enemy.' But I say to you, love your enemies, bless those who curse you, do good to those who hate you, and pray for those who spitefully use you and persecute you, that you may be sons of your Father in heaven; for He makes His sun rise on the evil and on the good, and sends rain on the just and on the unjust."* (Matthew 5:43-45 NKJV)

That is an anomaly that runs contrary to conventional wisdom and many are not able to bear it. Many cannot forgive and so have problems with the message of grace. The message of grace is the message of forgiveness. The God of grace is the God of forgiveness. If we are counting on God to forgive us, God is counting on us to forgive those who hurt us. I believe that is one of the hardest things that God has asked us to do. The mystery of grace is that it bestows mercy, kindness and forgiveness to an undeserving and often guilty person like you and me.

Heaven is only for the righteous, but Jesus has opened it for every sinner and every person who will just say to God, "I am sorry." Jesus said to the Father while on the cross suffering for the sins He did not commit, "Father, forgive them for they know not what they do" (Luke 23:34). He made it so simple that many of us think there's got to be more than just saying, "God, I'm so sorry." Many of us think that just saying those easy words is not enough for God to forgive people their sins and let them come into Heaven. They believe you must work extra hard, rid yourself of most, or at least somewhere between 50% and 70% of your sins, then God will add the rest, and grudgingly allow the sinner into His Presence.

That is not God's grace. That is human grace that says you pay part of your debt and your creditor forgives the rest. No, that is not God's grace. God's grace is 100% free because Jesus paid it all. You have nothing to contribute to your salvation while you are a sinner because it's free for you. However, after you have been saved, you receive the grace to serve God, and to do acceptable good deeds. Grace is truly a mystery because no one can fully understand the mind of God, who decided to have Jesus come down from Heaven and die to save a wretched, hopeless, disobedient, and sinful world like ours.

Many times I have wanted to take up issues with God about so many things in life, including the plan of salvation. There must have been better ways He could have done it without going through the terrible suffering and pain. Even with such costly sacrifice, people are still not convinced and others make a mockery of it. It is a mystery. I do not fully understand it and I do not think anybody else does either. That might explain why it is not fully emphasized much in the churches. Grace is not a natural human attribute or characteristic, it is God's characteristic. All humans fall short of the grace of God, and all are in need of grace. So it is difficult for pastors to explain what they do not know too much about. We are all recipients of God's grace and do not have special expertise in explaining it.

The Dispensation of Grace

Most of us have heard preachers talk about the dispensation of grace and then we are left to wonder: *What is dispensation?* A dispensation is a religious time frame or period that outlines God's rule and program of intervention in human history. It is set in order to orchestrate, direct, and accomplish His purpose on earth. For example, from creation to the time of Moses, God dealt with humans directly without intermediaries except for angels. During the period from Moses to the first coming of Christ, God gave the law and operated through the provisions of the law, and had Moses and the prophets dealing with man.

The period between Christ's first coming and His second coming is called the dispensation of grace. This is the period we are in now. It is the period when God reigns through Christ in the Holy Ghost. In this period of grace dispensation, God grants to man free access into His presence and the Throne of Grace that man may receive whatever he thinks about, asks for or imagines. Jesus said, "All things whatsoever you desire, when you pray, believe that you receive them and you shall have them" (Mark 11: 24). This period is when you and

I can receive anything from God free of charge, just for the asking. It is the period of complete freedom from restriction that was originally imposed on man because of the Adam and Eve's disobedience and the provisions of the law.

Those who believe are no longer under the law but under grace. "For sin shall not have dominion over you, for you are not under the law but under grace" (Romans 6:14). In theology, there seems to be a consensus that there are seven dispensations from creation to the time of Christ's rule on the earth.

These include the dispensation of:

- Innocence
- Conscience
- Human government
- Promise
- Law
- Grace
- Kingdom rule

This book is not about the theology of grace, but the reality, truth, practical implication, application, and power of the spirit of grace. That loving spirit will save, heal, deliver, provide, and transform lives and situations. This was the reason I started this book with my simple childhood stories. I wanted to show how God has showered His grace on the young and old, rich and poor, white and black, Jew and Gentile. God does not want us to continue in ignorance of the blessings and provisions of His grace.

And the times of ignorance God winked at; but now commands all men everywhere to repent: because He has appointed a day, in which He shall judge the world in righteousness, by that man whom He had ordained; whereof He had given assurance unto all men, in that He had raised Him from the dead. (Acts 17:30-31)

He certainly does not want us to be ignorant of this dispensation. Every dispensation is important and different, but this one seems to be the most important one because it is the culmination of previous dispensations. It is this dispensation wherein the Godhead or the Father, Son and the Holy Spirit, as One, becomes actively present in this world working to save everyone and not just the chosen people of Israel. This is the first time since the fall of Adam and Eve that salvation, healing, miracles, and blessings are free for all to partake. Now anybody can perform and/or receive miracles if he/she believes right from the first day of salvation. This is the first dispensation in which humans of all races can call upon God the Father directly.

We are actually living in a different period. There will never be another dispensation like this one in which God is literally begging people to come into His kingdom, giving general amnesty to even those who do not deserve it. To be very honest, most all of us do not. I believe that those who refuse this grace period will have only themselves to blame because it is said, "How shall we escape if we neglect so great a salvation" (Hebrews 2:3). God has paid the ultimate sacrifice for sin. There is no more sacrifice and there will be no other period of grace. "For if we sin willfully after we have received the knowledge of truth, there no longer remains any sacrifice for sin" (Hebrews 10: 26).

Salvation by Grace

One of the most important aspects of the dispensation of grace is the salvation and forgiveness of sin. They are obtained by grace and free of charge. Time was when you had to see a priest with a sin or peace offering before a sacrifice could be performed to atone for your sin. In the past, some denominations and organizations received gifts and presents to absolve people of their sins. Even today, it is possible to find places where such practices are still being used. He said, "There is none righteous, no, not one" (Roman 3:10). He also said, "The soul that sinneth, it shall die" (Ezekiel 18:4). Furthermore, in Romans 6:23 the Lord reiterated, "For the wages of sin is death but the gift of God is eternal life through Jesus Christ our Lord." From the human point of view, anyone who commits a crime that is punishable by the death penalty and is convicted is summarily executed. The same is true from God's point of view. In the Old Testament these laws were in force. But it does not happen this way in the New Testament. Why?

This is where the good news of the message of grace drew my attention. If you and I will be honest enough to tell ourselves the truth, there is probably something that we have done in our lifetime that is worthy of death. Someone may have thought, or may have entertained the idea, that we may deserve the death penalty. I do not know about you, but I have thought, said and done things that I would not like a second ear to hear. But God heard, saw and knew first hand all that I have gone through. So when He said that all have sinned and come short of the glory of God, I said, "Yes, Lord." The great thing about the message of grace that thrills me is that because of the grace of Jesus Christ, because of what Jesus suffered for me, my heavenly Father, is willing to forgive me for all of the messes I have made of my life, all the silly mistakes I have made, and those I will continue to make.

In Romans 5:20 we read, "Moreover the law entered, that the offence might abound. But where sin abounded, grace did much more abound." In other words, you cannot out sin the abundance of the grace that God has made available to those who believe and confess to Him; those who own up to their sins. Over and above that the scripture says, "There is, therefore, now no condemnation to those who are in Christ Jesus, who do not walk according to the flesh, but according to the Spirit. For the law of the Spirit of life in Christ Jesus has made me free from the law of sin and death" (Romans 8:1-2).

Salvation by grace means we can receive the free gift of the redemptive work of Christ for no money and at no cost to us. "Christ has redeemed us from the curse of the law, having been made a curse for us because as it is written, 'Cursed is everyone who hangs on a tree'" (Galatians 3:13). Jesus went to the cross to redeem and to save a lost humanity from the eternal punishment that was due us.

When you believe and accept Jesus as your Lord and Savior, you automatically become born again into the family and household of God. Jesus says that person, "has everlasting life, and shall not come into judgment (condemnation) but has passed from death to life" (John 5:24b). In Romans 6:23b we read, "...but the gift of God is eternal life through Jesus Christ our Lord." The grace of God brings eternal life to those who will receive it. It is free, praise God, it is free! Eternal life is free through the grace of Christ. You do not have to be righteous to receive salvation even though righteousness is your reward for accepting the grace of salvation. The thief on the cross was already dying in his sin, but even at the eleventh hour when he asked for mercy, he received grace which was the unmerited favor of God.

As you read this book, if you have not received the grace of salvation, just pause now and say this simple prayer:

Lord Jesus,
I believe you died for my sin.
I believe your death paid the full price for my sin.
I accept and receive You today as my Lord and Savior.
Come into my heart and give me your grace to become a child of God.
I now receive eternal life in your name.
Thank you.
Amen.

If you said this simple prayer wholeheartedly, it is done. You will begin to see the transformation in a matter of days as you continue to trust Him daily for the grace to live in your redeemed new life.

A classical example of the transforming power of the grace of God was the story of John Newton. His song, *Amazing Grace* says it all. The story behind the song is a classical example of a man who received grace. What was so amazing to him was that he knew he did not merit or deserve this grace and kindness that God was showing him when he was about to perish at sea with a ship load of slaves. This piece was taken from, "Amazing Grace: The Story of John Newton" by Al Rogers. The story can be read online at www.anointedlinks.com/amazing_grace.hmtl

It is important, dear friend, that we do not take the grace of God for granted, nor willfully reject our opportunity to receive the free gift of God now. "Behold now is the acceptable time; behold now is the day of salvation" (2 Corinthians 6:2b). God is willing and ready right now to forgive and save your soul from the wrath that will follow this period of grace. It will not last forever. Like past dispensations, it is for a time, a period or a definite duration.

The Joy of Living by Grace

The joy of living by grace is that you are happy, peaceful, and spiritually prosperous because you are no longer living in fear, anxiety, and worry. You know your life is no longer in your hands but in the hands of the Almighty God. You are happy because you know that those terrible things you may have committed in the past have all been forgiven, are washed away forever, and never to be remembered by God again. "As far as the east is from the west, so far has He removed our transgressions from us" (Psalm 103:12). The Word also says, "For I will forgive their iniquity, and will remember their sin no more" (Jeremiah 31:34). Those, who are under grace and not merely living by the law are continuously under the grace of forgiveness. When they sin and confess their sin, God forgives and wipes out their sin and they emerge as if the had never committed sin before. Of course that applies to everyone who genuinely confesses their sins.

God is not interested in our sin, but in our righteousness and sanctification. Since we cannot achieve righteousness by ourselves, God has made provision through Jesus Christ, for the forgiveness of sin for the whole world, for those who ask in repentance. The blood of Jesus makes them whole again. That is the power and beauty of the new dispensation of grace. Joy, peace and the hunger for righteousness follow everyone who receives the grace of salvation. The joy that follows repentance and salvation does not stop here on earth. Jesus said, "I say to you, likewise, there will be more joy in Heaven over one sinner who repents than over ninety-nine just persons who need no repentance" (Luke 15:7). The joy of living by grace is that you are at peace with yourself, God, and the host of heaven including God the Father, Son and Holy Spirit together with angels, archangels, the cherubim, and seraphim. All are rejoicing together with and for you. You become an instant celebrity in heaven. The joy of living by grace transcends anything you can think of or imagine. It is Heaven in your soul. It is peace in your mind. It is peace with other people, even those who have hurt you in the past.

Chapter 15

Grace to Change Your Circumstances

*T*here is grace for all situations. There is grace for sin and sinners, for living and dying, for when you are down and when you are on top of the world, grace to stand up against evil, and there is even grace to escape evil. There is grace to change a bad situation and grace to go through it. There is grace for every situation that can confront you because your God has gone ahead of you to prepare everything you will ever need or face in this life.

Grace to Lift You Up

I want to discuss the grace that will lift you up when you are down or facing a crisis of any type or proportion. Our God is Immanuel (God with us). He is the Almighty! He is the Alpha and the Omega, beginning and end, first and last, He who was, and is, and is to come. He is omnipotent, omnipresent, omniscient and omni-wealthy (if such a word exists). He is the God that makes impossibilities possible. He walked on the sea, divided the Red Sea and made it possible for His people to walk on dry ground. He closed the mouths of lions and made them become Daniel's friends while in the lion's den. He was the fourth person in the fire to protect Shadrach, Meshach and Abednego. He is the Lily of the Valley, the Rose of Sharon, the Bright and Morning Star.

Our God is the all-sufficient One. He is our great Provider; the ever faithful and True God. He is The Lord, our Healer. He is the God in the mountain and the God in the valley. He is the God of the night and the God of the daytime. He is the Everlasting and Ever-Living God. He is the Lord of our Peace, the Prince of Peace and our shelter in the time of trouble. He is the Lord of our Righteousness. He is the Lord our Shepherd, our Helper, Comforter, Rewarder, and Advocate.

The Lord is our very-present Help in time of need. He is the Lord of our Salvation, our Intercessor, and our High Priest. He is the Lamb of God that takes away the sins of the world. Our God is the King of kings and Lord of lords. He is the immortal, invisible, and invincible God. He is the Lion of the Tribe of Judah. One day with God is like a thousand years, and a thousand years are as a day. He has the whole world in His Hands. He is the covenant-keeping God. He is the divine and infinite intelligence. He is our Master and our friend.

Our God is the maker, owner, creator, and sustainer of heaven and earth. He is called Wonderful Counselor, Mighty God, and He is the Everlasting Father. He is the Holy Spirit, and the Father of Spirits, and so much, much more. The list is endless. Take just a few minutes and think about Him. What do *you* call Him? What do you *know* Him to be in *your* life?

You can even call Him by your own chosen name. Our God accepts honor, glory, praise and adoration, worship, adulation, and thanksgiving. His most common name is Jesus, the Savior. To experience spiritual, emotional, physical, and psychological uplifting, call on those hotlines or hot names. His name is hot in heaven and in the kingdom of darkness, but sweet and gentle in a believer's ear.

As you go through these names and call upon Him, whether in prayer or just reading through the names, you will experience an instant lift if you are feeling down in spirit. You can receive divine healing if you are calling to be healed of your affliction. You can receive grace for eternal salvation if you are not saved. Whatever the need is, God is more than sufficient. But remember, grace is given according to His will for you and not according to your wish at the time. God will not change a situation if it is serving His purpose. For instance, if giving you a particular gift will make you become proud, a thing God hates, He may not answer that prayer the way you may expect the answer. Read what the Apostle Paul said in Romans 12:7-9.

> *And lest I should be exalted above measure by the abundance of the revelations, a thorn in the flesh was given to me, a messenger of Satan to buffet me, lest I be exalted above measure. Concerning this thing, I pleaded with the Lord three times that it might depart from me. And He said to me, "My grace is sufficient for you, for my strength is made perfect in weakness." Therefore most gladly I will rather boast in my infirmities, that the power of Christ may rest upon me.*

There is abundant grace in all and any of the above names. John Newton, who was about to perish found grace and hope in Christ, and his life was changed to that of a happy, joyous preacher, and songwriter. You, too, will find peace, joy and contentment in God. I encourage you to read the biography of John Newton. It is an interesting read. When you are down in spirit or going through a tough time and need a lift, always remember that Jesus is the friend that sticks closer than a brother.

And let the peace of God rule in your hearts, to which also you were called in one body; and be thankful. Let the word of Christ dwell in you richly in all wisdom, teaching and admonishing one another in psalms and hymns and spiritual songs, singing with grace in your hearts to the Lord. And whatever you do in word or deed, do all in the name of the Lord Jesus, giving thanks to God the Father through Him. (Colossians 3:15-17)

The above passage says, "singing" with grace in your heart to the Lord." One of the most potent instruments of grace that the Lord uses to comfort and lift me up when I am down is by singing hymns of praise. When you sing, grace is released through the song lyrics, tune, and melody in your ear. A singing heart is a merry or joyful heart. Making music in your heart brings comfort and grace to bear upon your situation. It also has a cleansing and healing effect on the soul. Nobody captures the truth of this assertion as does Joseph Scriven in his lyrics, *"What a Friend We Have in Jesus."*

As you can see, people from ages past have used psalms, hymns, and spiritual songs to comfort and lift themselves and others from despair, anxiety, stressful circumstances, and illnesses. The Bible tells us of how young

David played tunes on his instruments to calm down King Saul when the crazy king had a tantrum or demonic attack.

Grace and Works Contrasted

There is a marked distinction between living by grace and living by your own righteousness. In living by grace righteousness is imputed to you, while living by your own works of righteousness is rejecting the gift of God's grace. In the former you receive grace and righteousness by faith and enjoy all its free benefits, rights and privileges that the death and resurrection of Jesus Christ bought. While working and living by your own righteousness, you are functioning under the law and not under grace.

As we have seen in earlier passages, grace supersedes the law but does not abolish it. If you choose to live under the law, you are obligated by the law to fulfill over 6,000 laws written in the scriptures, including those written in your own heart. This is because the scripture says, "For whoever shall keep the whole law, and yet stumble in one *point*, he is guilty of all. For He who said, 'Do not commit adultery,' also said, 'Do not murder.' Now if you do not commit adultery, but you do murder, you have become a transgressor of the law" (James 2:10-11 NKJV). Those who live under the law shall be judged by the spirit of the law, and those who live under grace shall be judged by the law of grace.

> *For the law of the Spirit of life in Christ Jesus has made me free from the law of sin and death. For what the law could not do in that it was weak through the flesh, God did by sending His own Son in the likeness of sinful flesh, and for sin: He condemned sin in*

the flesh, that the righteous requirement of the law might be fulfilled in us who do not walk according to the flesh but according to the Spirit. (Romans 8:2-4)

As I read these words and weighed both options, I have chosen to live by grace. I do not know about you, but the difference is clear. It is up to you. I *am* a child of grace. I live, move, and have my being in the grace of God Almighty. It is grace that brought me here, it is grace that keeps me and it is grace that will lead me home.

The purpose of grace is that we share in God's divine nature while living in this world of sin and not be affected by it. When Jesus was in the world, He lived among sinners, ate with them, and hung out with them. He touched them and they thronged Him, and yet the Bible says that He was without sin (Hebrew 4:15). That is the kind of life that Christ came to give us. He wants to make us live in this world, yet not be stained by the sins and wickedness therein. This is not something an individual can do through his or her self-righteousness. Isaiah 64:6 says, "But we are all like an unclean thing, and all our righteousness are like filthy rags; we all fade as a leaf, and our iniquities, like the wind, have taken us away."

God is not interested in our self-righteousness, but in the righteousness that is through His Son, Jesus Christ. Does this make you relax or does it make you sit on edge? If it makes you sit on edge, you may be relying more heavily on your self- righteousness than on the righteousness of grace. The righteousness of grace is received by faith and not by works, not even by fasting and prayer.

Grace and Love

Grace, mercy, and kindness are the result of outward manifestations of love that God has for us. Grace works with love. Where there is no love, there is hardly any redeeming grace, because grace bestows unmerited and undeserved blessing and favor on the recipient. John 3:16 says, "For God so loved the world that He gave His only begotten Son, that whoever believes in Him should not perish but have everlasting life." God was demonstrating His love for a lost humanity when He decided to come and live on earth as one of us. In love there is grace and where there is no love there is no grace.

Equally so, in love there is compassion. Compassion is a strong feeling of sympathy for people who are suffering and there is a strong desire to assist them. In God's compassion, He released His grace that dispenses empathy, kindness, leniency, tenderness, and feelings of sympathy, forgiveness, understanding, warmness, love, blessing, and friendship. We have many feelings of compassion because God gave us those feelings out of His great love. He loves so much that He is willing to do anything to redeem and help you. Over and above everything else, God continues to give. He left us His Holy Spirit to guide and comfort us through the vagaries of this life.

God loves you in a way that you will never fully know or understand. He is for you and not against you. He says, "I know the thoughts (plans) I have toward you, says the Lord, thoughts of peace and not of evil, to give you a future and a hope" (Jeremiah 29:11). God's heartbeat for you is to give you the best according to His plan and purpose for your life. It's not always according to your wishes or the wishes of others. He wants to communicate His peace, love, joy, and health to you and show you the bedrock of human existence. Without these, life is miserable, irrespective of your status.

Love is the motive behind God's grace upon your life. However, love demands reciprocity. In other words, love is reciprocal. When God stretches out His love to you, reach out and receive it. "You shall love the Lord your God with all your heart, with all your soul and with all your mind (might)" (Matthew 22:37). Love begets love. Not only does God expect your love, He needs it as much as you need His. When you respond to God in love, He will shower you with much more amazing love and spiritual blessings. Loving God and receiving His grace is the greatest thing in all our lives.

Grace for All Eternity

As we have seen previously, there are different types of grace but there is one that we have not given any attention to yet. It is called the gift or grace of eternal life.

What shall it profit a man if he shall gain the whole world and lose his soul or what shall a man give in exchange for His soul. (Mark 8:36)

"The gift of God is eternal life through Jesus Christ our Lord" (Romans 3:23b). God intends for us to be wise with our gifts and graces and to invest them in things that have eternal value. When we do good works, we are investing in eternal life. The work that God would want us to do in order to inherit eternal life is to believe in His Son. Grace for eternity is given to those who believe in Jesus Christ, the Son of the Living God.

> *Then they said unto Him, "What shall we do that we might do the work of God?" Jesus answered and said to them, "This is the work of God that you believe on Him whom He has sent."* (John 6:28-29)

> *He that believes in Him is not condemned; but he that does not believe is condemned already, because he has not believed in the name of the only begotten Son of God.* (John 3:18)

Jesus Christ is God manifested and personified in the flesh. Eternal life is in Him just as mortal life was in Him also. Because Jesus had life in Himself, He was able to give life to a number of dead people who believed and had faith in Him when He was here on earth. "Jesus said… I am the resurrection and the life: he who believes in me, though he may die, he shall live. And whoever lives and believes in me shall never die. Do you believe this" (John 11:25-26). This is a very powerful and profound statement that everyone needs to take seriously. Jesus backed up this claim by raising Lazarus, who had been dead and in the grave for four days. Even Jesus rose from the dead after three days.

He has eternal life in Himself and has promised to give it to those who believe in Him, just as He gave physical or mortal life to those that needed it, and believed in Him while He was here on earth. He made an incredible claim and those who were very close to Him confirmed that claim. Read what the disciple John had to say about Jesus.

> *And this is the testimony: that God has given us eternal life, and this life is in His Son. He who has the Son has life; he who does not have the Son of*

God does not have life. These things I have written to you who believe in the name of the Son of God, that you may know that you have eternal life, and that you may continue to believe in the name of the Son of God. (1 John 5:11-13)

We have already seen that grace and truth came from Jesus. Now we see that eternal life is in Him because He was, and is, and will always be God. Because He is God, He wants to give us eternal life for free.

Would you like to be a part of that? To Jesus, giving you eternal life is as easy as giving you air for free. I know it sounds incredible to some people and if it does, it means He is God because only God does incredible and unbelievable things. He asks you not to fear and instead to just believe. You have the opportunity to trust Him and believe His Word or risk spending eternity without Him if things turn out that He is who He claims to be. However, by that time it will be much too late to change anything because death may have already claimed you.

Grace for eternity is real and freely available just for the asking. Whoever does not believe the Word of the scriptures and the testimony of God's saints would probably not believe even if an angel came down from Heaven to speak with them either. The beauty of the message of grace is that it guarantees a high quality of life here on earth. It also leads to eternity after this life.

I invite you to add the grace of eternal life to the many other graces you have already received from God. The God that has the power to give life and to take it away also has power to give eternal life. Just as you have accepted the other graces we have discussed in this book, grace for eternal life is greater than all those put together, and you really have nothing to lose except your fear of death. The fear of death all experience is not the fear of sleeping into death, but the fear of eternal death and separation from God. The fear of death is the only fear you will lose when you receive the grace of eternal life found in Jesus Christ. I encourage you to make that decision now by saying that simple prayer we talked about earlier. God bless you as you take your next step into faith.

For those who have already made the decision, God bless you. "As you have therefore received Christ Jesus the Lord, walk in Him, rooted and built up (grounded) in Him and established in the faith, as you have been taught, abounding in it with thanks giving" (Colossians 2:3-4). The grace of our Lord Jesus Christ, and the love of God, and the communion of the Holy Spirit be with you now.

Grace to Change Circumstances

The changes that will be beneficial to you all start from within. In order to change your life and circumstances, you must begin by changing the way you think. Your thinking pattern determines your actions. Thoughts are a very powerful, spiritual energy that easily materialize into the concrete, material or physical equivalence. Every thought that is acted upon produces a replica in the natural state. Therefore, it is important to understand the process by which you can change your circumstances and situations.

We take our thoughts for granted, but they affect every single thing we do in this world. They affect our very being, existence and our future. Our thinking pattern should be futuristic even though we live in the present. This is because we live our life in seconds, and seconds are fleeting moments of time that pass as soon as they appear. It is very possible to dwell on our thoughts in the past more than when we activate our thinking toward the future. There is a big difference between thoughts and thinking. Thoughts are about things and impulses that are past, while thinking is about things in the present or future. The pattern of thoughts determines whether we can easily change our situation, or not.

When we dwell on our thoughts hopefully they have changed our situation for the better. But because they were not always good, we merely recycled our thoughts and they become unproductive. If we do a lot of thinking, most times we come up with fresh new ideas that will help us change our situation. Those who receive grace to change their situation think progressively. They know that thoughts and impulses expire as quickly as they come.

When we are not actively thinking that is when the mind comes up with its own thought processes. The mind never sits idle. It is always engaged, even when we are sleeping. It never sleeps. It draws inspiration and subjects from the spirit and from the environment. It generates billions of thoughts on its own. The mind's database is infinite and it has the ability through the subconscious mind to draw from the Divine and Infinite Intelligence.

Grace is a spiritual, intangible gift from above that works through the mind to manifest into its physical equipollence. To change a situation you must tap the wisdom, knowledge, and power from your spirit through the conscious and subconscious mind. Delving into the spirit or the subconscious is where many people have problems, because they do not want to take the time, effort, and necessary sacrifice. You must begin to think from your inner mind to be able to tap resources that are not readily available in the natural world. All solutions for difficult problems are achieved from inner consciousness and resources. These take time, reflection, and perseverance in which most people would rather not invest. Every successful person has drawn from this vast inner resource of life at one point or another.

It takes effort and practice to draw repeatedly from there. When a situation or problem confronts you and there is no ready or available solution in the natural state, you must realize that there are solutions in the unseen spiritual world. Everything is available, overflowing with power and is possible there. When I say everything, I mean every thing. There is no lack or shortage in the Divine mind or His mind. There is no competition in the Divine mind. There is no sickness in the Divine mind. There is only super abundance in the Divine mind. That is why Jesus said, "I am come that they might have life and have it more abundantly" (John 10:10).

Every sickness has a cure, every problem has a solution, and every body part has a spare. There is nothing under the sun that does not have a solution. The only limiting factor is our level of thinking and imagination. Another limitation is the lack of faith to call on those things that are not, as though they are present. That is calling forth the solution from the realm of the spirit. When Adam was created he was a dual being. He could see in the physical world and in the spiritual world. He could see and hear God clearly. He interacted with God and the animals one on one. But when he fell out of God's grace, he was driven out of the Eden, and lost most of those spiritual qualities. His sight was then reduced to only physical things, and that was when he saw that he was naked.

His spiritual side became second nature, instead of being first nature. His spiritual nature went underground.

It did not disappear completely, but God made it more difficult for him to access it with ease. That was also when he lost fellowship with God. It was never recorded that Adam ever saw God or spoke with Him directly again. God is spirit, and they that wish to see Him must see Him through the spirit or rather with the eyes of the spirit. The ability to see things in the spirit or with the inner eye is called inspiration or visualization. The ability to change or effect things in the spirit is called faith. Everybody has a measure of those gifts.

When you combine faith and inspiration you produce what I call *faith-inspiration*. Faith-inspiration is the ability to see a thing in the spirit and capture it in the natural state. This ability comes with commitment, perseverance, and inward focus. As big as these words sound, they are easily mobilized.

A quick example would be when you are studying for a driver's license test. As you study you concentrate, persevere, dedicate, and visualize. Visualizing the road gives you the inspiration, and inspiration produces confidence. If you cannot visualize the road networks properly, you may not have enough confidence to drive under supervision.

This unique ability is imprinted in our minds. That is why whatever we sincerely and truly desire, ardently and earnestly believe, painstakingly and passionately pursue with faith and inspiration, will become a reality. Whether it is a solution to a problem, an answer to a nagging question, the healing of the body or any other of life's challenges, it will turn around. Faith-inspiration comes only by grace: it is a gift of grace.

Many people see things in the spirit but are not able to capture them in the natural world, while others have natural abilities but have a hard time articulating things in the spirit. Those who harness their faith-inspiration are creative problem solvers.

Inspiration is always laden with passion, hope, and possibilities. Once you are inspired to do something, you also have hope of its success. However, success is determined by how clearly you visualize, and the sustaining power of your faith and passion. The grace to change a situation demands your total commitment and full attention. All things are possible to him that believes. The grace to change your situation is already with you. The scripture says, "The word is near you, even in your mouth and in your heart that is the word of faith which we preach" (Romans 9:8).

Chapter 16

The Grace Chapter

*G*race is mentioned in almost every book of the Bible from Genesis to Revelation. Here are some interesting and uplifting passages of scripture to increase your knowledge of grace. By reading these scriptures may you be lifted in grace, and may you find those passages that will change your life for good.

Grace scriptures include, but are not limited to these:

2 Corinthians 12:9 - "And he said unto me, my grace is sufficient for thee: for my strength is made perfect in weakness. Most gladly therefore will I rather glory in my infirmities, that the power of Christ may rest upon me."

Genesis 6: 8 - "But Noah found grace in the eyes of the LORD."

Exodus 22: 27 "For that *is* his only covering, it *is* his garment for his skin. What will he sleep in? And it will be that when he cries to Me, I will hear, for I *am* gracious.

Exodus 33:19 - Then He said, "I will make all My goodness pass before you, and I will proclaim the name of the Lord before you. I will be gracious to whom I will be gracious, and I will have compassion on whom I will have compassion."

Exodus 34:6 " And the Lord passed by before him, and proclaimed, The Lord, The Lord God, merciful and gracious, longsuffering, and abundant in goodness and truth."

Psalms 45:2 - "Thou art fairer than the children of men; grace is poured into thy lips; therefore God hath blessed thee for ever."

Psalms 84:11 - "The Lord is a sun and shield; the lord will give grace and glory; no good thing will be withheld from those who walk uprightly."

Nehemiah 9:17 "But You *are* God, Ready to pardon, Gracious and merciful, Slow to anger, Abundant in kindness, And did not forsake them."

2Chronicles 30:9 "...for the Lord your God is gracious and merciful, and will not turn away his face from you, if ye return unto him."

The Grace Chapter

Hosea 14:2 "Take with you words, and turn to the Lord: say unto him, Take away all iniquity, and receive us graciously: so will we render the calves of our lips."

Isaiah 30:18 "Therefore the Lord will wait, that He may be gracious to you; And therefore He will be exalted, that He may have mercy on you. For the Lord *is* a God of justice; Blessed *are* all those who wait for Him."

Amos 5:15 "Hate evil, love good; Establish justice in the gate. It may be that the Lord God of hosts will be gracious to the remnant of Joseph."

…**Jonah 4:2** "for I know that You *are* a gracious and merciful God, slow to anger and abundant in lovingkindness, One who relents from doing harm."

Zechariah 4:7 - "Who art thou, O great mountain? Before Zerubbabel thou shalt become a plain; and he shall bring forth the headstone thereof with shoutings, crying, Grace, grace unto it."

Zechariah 12: 10 - "And I will pour out on the house of David and on the inhabitants of Jerusalem the spirit of grace and supplication…"

Luke 2:20 - "And the child grew, and waxed strong in spirit, filled with wisdom; and the grace of God was upon him."

John 1:17 - "For the law was given by Moses, but grace and truth came by Jesus Christ."

Acts 13:43 - "... continue in the grace of God."

Acts 14: 3 - "... His grace granting signs and wonders to be done by their hands."

Acts 14: 26 - "... Commended to the grace of God."

Romans 1:7 - "To all in Rome, beloved of God, called to be saints: grace to you and peace from God our Father and the Lord Jesus Christ."

Romans 3:24 - "Being justified freely by his grace through the redemption that is in Christ Jesus..."

Romans 5:15 - "But the free gift is not like the offence. For if by the one man's offence many died, much more the grace of God and the gift by the grace of the one man, Jesus Christ, abounded to many."

Romans 5:17 - "For if by the one man's offense death reigned through the one, much more those who receive abundance of grace and of the gift of righteousness will reign in life through the One, Jesus Christ."

Romans 6: 14 - "For sin shall not have dominion over you for you are not under the law but under grace."

Romans 12:3 - "For I say, through the grace given unto me, to every man that is among you, not to think of himself more highly than he ought to think; but to think soberly, according as God hath dealt to every man the measure of faith."

Romans 15:15 - "Nevertheless, brethren I have written more boldly to you in some points, as reminding you, because of the grace given to me by God."

Romans 16:20 - "And the God of grace will crush Satan under your feet shortly. The grace of our Lord Jesus Christ be with you. Amen."

1 Corinthians 1:3 - "Grace to you and peace from God our Father and the Lord Jesus Christ."

1 Corinthians 15:10 - "But by the grace of God I am what I am; and His grace which was bestowed upon me was not in vain; but I labored more abundantly than they all: yet not I, but the grace of God which was with me."

1 Corinthians 16:23 - "The grace of our Lord Jesus Christ be with you."

2 Corinthians 1:2 - "Grace be to you and peace from God our Father, and from the Lord Jesus Christ."

2 Corinthians 4:15 - "For all things are for your sakes, that the abundant grace might through the thanksgiving of many rebound to the glory of God."

2 Corinthians 9:8 - "And God is able to make all grace abound toward you, that you, always having all sufficiency in all things, may abound to every good work."

2 Corinthians 9:14 - "And by their prayer for you, which long after you for the exceeding grace of God in you."

2 Corinthians 12:9 - "And he said unto me, my grace is sufficient for thee: for my strength is made perfect in weakness. Most gladly therefore will I rather glory in my infirmities, that the power of Christ may rest upon me."

2 Corinthians 13:14 - "The grace of the Lord Jesus Christ, and the love of God, and the communion of the Holy Ghost, be with you all. Amen."

Galatians 1:3 - "Grace to you and peace from God the Father, and from our Lord Jesus Christ."

Galatians 2:21 - "I do not frustrate the grace of God: for if righteousness comes by the law, then Christ is dead in vain."

Galatians 5:4 - "Christ is become of no effect unto you, whosoever of you are justified by the law; ye are fallen from grace."

Galatians 6:18 - "Brethren, the grace of our Lord Jesus Christ be with your spirit. Amen."

Ephesians 1:2 - "Grace to you, and peace, from God our Father, and from the Lord Jesus Christ."

Ephesians 2:8 - "For by grace are ye saved through faith; and that not of yourselves; it is the gift of God."

Ephesians 4:7 - "But unto every one of us is given grace according to the measure of the gift of Christ."

Ephesians 6:24 - "Grace be with all them that love our Lord Jesus Christ in sincerity. Amen."

Philippians 1:2 - "Grace be unto you, and peace, from God our Father, and from the Lord Jesus Christ."

Philippians 4:23 - "The grace of our Lord Jesus Christ be with you all. Amen."

Colossians 1:2 - "To the saints and faithful brethren in Christ which are at Colosse; Grace be unto you, and peace, from God our Father and the Lord Jesus Christ."

Colossians 4:18 - "The salutation by the hand of me, Paul. Remember my bonds. Grace be with you. Amen."

1 Thessalonians 1:1 – "Paul, and Silvanus, and Timotheus, unto the church of the Thessalonians which is in God the Father and in the Lord Jesus Christ; Grace be unto you, and peace, from God our Father, and the Lord Jesus Christ."

1 Thessalonians 5:28 - "The grace of our Lord Jesus Christ be with you. Amen."

2 Thessalonians 1:2 - "Grace unto you, and peace, from God our Father and the Lord Jesus Christ."

2 Thessalonians 3:18 - "The grace of our Lord Jesus Christ be with you all. Amen."

1 Timothy 1:2 - "Unto Timothy, my own son in the faith: Grace, mercy, and peace, from God our Father and Jesus Christ our Lord."

1 Timothy 6:21 - "Which some professing have erred concerning the faith. Grace be with thee. Amen."

2 Timothy 1:2 - "The Lord Jesus Christ be with thy spirit. Grace be with you. Amen."

Titus 1:4 - "To Titus, mine own son after the common faith; Grace, mercy, and peace, from God the Father and the Lord Jesus Christ our Saviour."

Titus 2:11 - "For the grace of God that bringeth salvation hath appeared to all men…"

The Grace Chapter

Titus 3:7 - "That being justified by his grace, we should be made heirs according to the hope of eternal life."

Titus 3:15 - "All that are with me salute thee. Greet them that love us in the faith. Grace be with you all. Amen."

Philemon 3 - "Grace to you, and peace, from God our Father and the Lord Jesus Christ."

Philemon 2:5 - "The grace of our Lord Jesus Christ be with your spirit. Amen."

Hebrews 2:9 - "But we see Jesus, who was made a little lower than the angels for the suffering of death, crowned with glory and honour; that He by the grace of God should taste death for every man."

Hebrews 4:16 - "Let us therefore come boldly unto the throne of grace, that we may obtain mercy, and find grace to help in time of need."

Hebrews 10:29 - "Of how much sorer punishment, suppose ye, shall he be thought worthy, who hath trodden under foot the Son of God, and hath counted the blood of the covenant, wherewith he was sanctified, an unholy thing, and hath done despite unto the Spirit of grace?"

Hebrew 12:15 - "Looking diligently lest any man fail of the grace of God; lest any root of bitterness springing up trouble you, and thereby many be defiled."

Hebrews 12:28 - "Wherefore we receiving a kingdom which cannot be moved, let us have grace, whereby we may serve God acceptably with reverence and godly fear."

Hebrews 13:9 - "Be not carried about with diverse and strange doctrines. For it is a good thing that the heart be established with grace; not with meats, which have not profited them that have been occupied therein."

Hebrews 13:25 - "Grace be with you all. Amen."

James 4:6 - "But he giveth more grace. Wherefore he saith, God resisteth the proud, but giveth grace unto the humble."

1 Peter 1:2 - "Elect according to the foreknowledge of God the Father, through sanctification of the Spirit, unto obedience and sprinkling of the blood of Jesus Christ; Grace unto you, and peace, be multiplied."

1 Peter 2:3 - "If so be ye have tasted that the Lord is gracious."

1 Peter 3:7 - "Likewise, ye husbands, dwell with them according to knowledge, giving honor unto the wife, as unto the weaker vessel, and as being

The Grace Chapter

heirs together of the grace of life; that your prayers be not hindered."

1 Peter 5:5 - "Likewise you younger people, submit yourselves to your elders. Yes, all of you be submissive to one another, and be clothed with humility, for God resists the proud, but gives grace to the humble."

1 Peter 5: 10 - "But may the God of all grace, who called us to His eternal glory by Christ Jesus, after you have suffered a while, perfect, establish, strengthen, and settle you."

1 Peter 5:12 - "By Silvanus, a faithful brother unto you, as I suppose, I have written briefly, exhorting, and testifying that this is the true grace of God wherein ye stand."

2 Peter 1:2 - "Grace and peace be multiplied unto you through the knowledge of God, and of Jesus our Lord."

2 Peter 3:18 - "But grow in grace, and in the knowledge of our Lord and Saviour Jesus Christ. To Him be glory both now and forever. Amen."

2 John 3 - "Grace be with you, mercy, and peace, from God the Father, and from the Lord Jesus Christ, the Son of the Father, in truth and love."

Revelation 1:4 - "John to the seven churches which are in Asia; Grace be unto you, and peace, from Him which is, and which was, and which is to come; and from the seven Spirits which are before his throne."

Revelation 22:21 - "The grace of our Lord Jesus Christ be with you all. Amen."

The End

Other Books by the author:
The Authority of the Excellent Name of Jesus

ABOUT THE BOOK

"*I* feel Humphrey Akparah has placed a lot of deep thought and emotional concern in his decision to write about God's grace in this book. He defines grace, provides many examples of grace, looks at grace from many angles, shows that grace is ever present and backs it up with many Bible quotations so that anyone, who doubts its presence, has the opportunity to look into the Scriptures and find those quotations for him/herself.

He makes grace a very simple and uncomplicated source of power which can be obtained by each and every person who desires it. He/she only has to believe in God and ask for His grace through Jesus Christ. He explains thoroughly why you cannot earn grace. You must ask for it, but only God can provide it. And God decides who receives His grace, when he/she receives it and for what purpose it is given. He shows God's grace was present at the beginning of time, is present today and will continue to exist until the end of time. Everybody, who would like to receive God's grace, should read this book and find out how easily it can be discovered. Anyone, who would like to receive the full richness of God's abiding grace, should read this book in its entirety to find out how easily it will be revealed."

Rod Woolridge

ABOUT THE AUTHOR

Humphrey Akparah is a spiritual counselor and teacher, motivational speaker, author and a deliverance minister. As a church planter, he founded two churches in Nigeria and was instrumental in other church planting and equipping. He is graced with the gift of spiritual insight and discernment into spiritual problems. He is a Canadian citizen and currently resides in Alberta, worshipping at the House of Praise of the Redeemed Christian Church of God, Calgary.

Author

CPSIA information can be obtained at www.ICGtesting.com
Printed in the USA
LVOW131952220413

330357LV00002B/11/P